ILLUSTRATIONS OF THE LITURGY

S. JOHN'S CHURCH, NEWCASTLE.

By the kindness of Messrs. Mowbray the Alcuin Club here reproduces the frontispiece of the English Churchman's Kalendar for the year 1912. The photograph by Mr. Cyril Ellis represents, through the courtesy of the Rev. Cyril Hepher, M.A., the Vicar, the principal altar of S. John's Church, designed by Sir Charles Nicholson, Bart., F.R.I.B.A. This altar is shown as a fine example of a typical Holy Table with a reredos of tabernacle work, in contrast to the dorsals which are represented in the body of this volume.

𝔄𝔩𝔠𝔲𝔦𝔫 𝔠𝔩𝔲𝔟 𝔠𝔬𝔩𝔩𝔢𝔠𝔱𝔦𝔬𝔫𝔰

XIX

ILLUSTRATIONS OF THE LITURGY

BEING THIRTEEN DRAWINGS OF THE CELEBRATION OF THE HOLY COMMUNION IN A PARISH CHURCH

BY

CLEMENT O. SKILBECK

With Notes descriptive and explanatory, and an Introduction on " The Present Opportunity," by
PERCY DEARMER, D.D.

A. R. MOWBRAY & CO. LTD.
LONDON : 28 Margaret Street, Oxford Circus, W.
OXFORD : 9 High Street
MILWAUKEE, U.S.A. : THE YOUNG CHURCHMAN CO.

First impression, 1912

CONTENTS

LANTERN SLIDES

The Committee of the Alcuin Club has been asked to prepare lantern slides of the illustrations in this book, in order that the book may thus be used to supply notes for a lantern-lecture. These slides can be hired from the Hon. Sec., Alcuin Club, 102 Adelaide Road, London, N.W., for the sum of 3 shillings the set, with 1 shilling for insurance and postage. A few extra slides are added to this set.

Other slides are noted at the end of this volume.

ILLUSTRATIONS OF THE LITURGY

INTRODUCTION

THE PRESENT OPPORTUNITY

IN the year of the Coronation of King George V many must have learnt how beautiful an Anglican Service can be if only the Anglican rules are adhered to. The rite in Westminster Abbey last June was so impressive because it was not spoilt by that traditional slovenliness and inadequacy, which obscure the character of other collegiate or cathedral services.[1] Had the King been anointed and

[1] At a slight risk perhaps of being misunderstood, I here subjoin a criticism which, overstated though it be, does yet give vent to an opinion, that, as the reader will know, is very common among artists and writers. There is a deep-rooted notion in the Church that the so-called "moderate" compromise of the cathedral type, though admittedly indefensible on principle (while the Prayer Book remains as it is), yet is necessary because the nation will not be patient of any other—that the nation in fact likes it. The truth would rather seem to be that the nation tolerates but does not admire this compromise, and is chilled by a certain drab formality and an absence of the atmosphere of prayer in our cathedrals; because people need sympathy, and breadth of outlook, rather than that merely negative moderatism of which the Church has had so much. At any rate the following quotation from a well-known novelist (and just now our popular novelists are our popular preachers) will at least serve to suggest the possibility that the nation may be growing to like this type of service less every year :—

"He had already established a fund to provide for the education of the deans and chapters of the cathedrals, with a view to prevent in the future a recurrence of the hideous artistic mistakes made by these dignitaries in the discharge of their respective offices. He had noticed, as a good many other people of discrimination do daily, that the moment a dignitary of an English cathedral opens his mouth either to read, to sing, or to pray, the divine influences engendered by the architecture and the hallowed associations of the building, and by the music of the choir are rather more than neutralized, and sensitive worshippers of God through the medium of art go away shocked: so he had determined to make an effort to prevent the continuance of so gross a state of things. It was also his hope to produce by a conference of poets, who were also literary men, a Church Hymnal which should be worthy of being regarded as poetry, in place of the doggerel, ancient and modern, which

crowned in accordance with the usual ceremonial compromise, how mean and meagre the ecclesiastical side of the
function would have appeared! But on the occasion of a
Coronation the English Church has always awoke from her
æsthetic lethargy, and even in the worst times has risen
to the effort of carrying out a great part of the Ornaments
Rubric. So it was this year—with many added touches of
beauty which came to the Abbey from the liturgical revival
of our time: no laws were wholly broken, no rubrics wholly
disregarded, the service in the main was rendered faithfully
to the English Use; and as a consequence every beholder,
of every nation and form of religion, was stirred and
impressed. Nor was this all. The whole nation, nonconformist as well as conformist, was satisfied—nay, it was
delighted, touched, kindled. People who generally object
to beauty in connection with the worship of God made no
objection on this occasion—partly, no doubt, because they
are used to ceremonial in connection with royal functions,
but partly also because they knew that it all was lawful
and done under authority: indeed the two reasons overlap
—such public ceremonial must, they know, be lawful, and
they never dream of questioning it. There is no slur of
"disloyalty" about such ceremonial; and the English nation
loves it exceedingly. Now, in the case of many parish
churches, it is precisely this slur, not undeserved, that
has largely prevented the Church Revival from estab-
lishing itself in the hearts of the English people.

If the Church of England to herself would be but true!
Here was an occasion on which she was; an occasion on
which little was omitted, and nothing without authority
interpolated; an occasion on which the Ornaments Rubric
was observed—and the result was a service which the
Church of England could set before the whole world,
for the whole world to respect and admire. No other part
of Christ's Church could have done it better, if so well.

cannot but be offensive to a heaven which has endowed men—some men—
with ears sensitive to a false rhyme, a ridiculous metre, and a mixed meta-
phor. And he was sanguine enough to hope that, by the introduction of an
element of culture (reasonably endowed) the Church might eventually produce a poet."— Frankfort Moore, *The Food of Love*.

Indeed, where else could it have been done so well? For here was a ceremonial majestic, even gorgeous, and yet simple all the way, and speaking simply to the hearts of men; and here was a ritual written in our great vernacular, for all to understand, for all to love, as its stately phrases echoed in their hearts, and still will echo in many a heart for years to come. Some of the phrases peculiar to the Coronation Service are indeed among the noblest epigrams of all literature : such as this, which is accompanied by the ceremonial of the girding with the Sword :

"With this Sword do justice, stop the growth of iniquity, protect the holy Church of God, help and defend widows and orphans, restore the things that are gone to decay, maintain the things that are restored, punish and reform what is amiss, and confirm what is in good order: that doing these things you may be glorious in all virtue; and so faithfully serve our Lord Jesus Christ in this life, that you may reign for ever with him in the life which is to come."

Or this, at the ceremonial of the delivery of the Sceptre with the Dove :

"Be so merciful that you be not too remiss ; so execute justice that you forget not mercy. Punish the wicked, protect and cherish the just, and lead your people in the way wherein they should go."

The later additions are as English prose not less admirable : such is Sancroft's—"When you see this Orb thus set under the Cross, remember that the whole world is subject to the Power and Empire of Christ our Redeemer."

And this, at the ceremonial of the Presenting of the Holy Bible, which dates from the Revolution :

"Our gracious King; we present you with this Book, the most valuable thing that this world affords. Here is wisdom ; this is the royal Law ; these are the lively Oracles of God."

And the Eucharistic Service itself, in which the Coronation rites are imbedded, the Service which is used day after day in all our churches, what can rival it for beauty of diction? Many are busy searching for faults just now with

a view to revision ; and faults there are, just as there are
faults in the Latin Canon of the Mass, which is indeed
such a skein of confusion that scholars have not yet succeeded
in disentangling it, and which is dry and jejune as compared
with the Eastern rites. The English Liturgy is in some
points inferior to the older services of both East and West,
as it is to the Scottish and American Liturgies [1] But it
shares with these last, and with the English Bible that forms
so large a part of our services, this peculiar distinction ·—
the language in which it is written is a language at
the finest point of its development, whereas both Greek
and Latin service-books belong to a language that was
past its prime. And to this must be added the fact that,
when the Prayer Book is obeyed, as it was at the Coronation,
the Ornaments Rubric fixes our ceremonial as well as our
ritual at a point before the abounding degradation of a *rococo*
period had set in.[2]

Here, at the Sacring of King George V, was, in fact,
all the gain of the Reformation, with almost none of its
losses [2]—none, rather, of those losses inflicted by the individualism of subsequent generations upon that Reformation
Settlement, which was set forth in the first English Prayer
Book and enshrined as a legal enactment for us still
by the Ornaments Rubric

[1] When the English Prayer Book is revised, there can be no doubt that the
English Liturgy will by general consent be approximated to the Scottish and
to that of the First English Prayer Book, by the removal of these acknow-
ledged blemishes

[2] For the Ornaments Rubric, see the Report of the Sub Committee of the
Upper House of the Convocation of Canterbury, No 416, *The Ornaments of
the Church and its Ministers*, S P C K , 1908   Also the Aleuin Club Tract,
No 1, *The Ornaments of the Rubric*, by J T Micklethwaite. Also W. H
Frere, *The Principles of Religious Ceremonial*, Longmans, 1906, cap xiv   Also
F. C Eeles, *The Ornaments Rubric* ; Mowbrays (Churchman's Penny
Library), 1908

[3] The Coronation Service was much altered in 1685, and in the eighteenth
and nineteenth centuries most, perhaps all, liturgiologists would prefer to
see it in great measure restored to the form which survived till after the
Restoration See, e g , Leopold G Wickham Legg, *Suggestions for the
Reconstruction of the Coronation Ceremonies* (Church Historical Society. No.
LXVII). London, S P C K , 1902   There were some more obvious defects
The bishops, for instance, did not wear their mitres, which they could law-
fully have used

What I have here said about the Coronation Service is equally true of the Eucharist which is celebrated in every cathedral and parish church. The King's Sacring is itself part of a solemn celebration of the Holy Communion; and in every Eucharist there is the same glory of language, and there should be a similar beauty of presentment, if only the law were equally well observed. This is what the whole Anglican Communion might rise to, can rise to, by the simple expedient of being true to itself.

If only it had been thus true during recent generations!

The curse of the English Church, and indeed of the whole Anglican Communion, has been the individualism of its members. They have been a law unto themselves; and yet this individualism has seldom had the justification of originality: sometimes it has been Geneva that was copied, sometimes Rome. The result has been that our Church has failed to make herself recognizable: foreigners know almost nothing about her, have no idea what she is like, would not recognize her when they saw her.

Herein lies the practical importance of externals. It has been the fashion to despise them, because the modern Anglo-Saxon, till quite recent times, has in his soul despised art and disliked sacramentalism. But, as a mere matter of practical statesmanship, externals cannot be ignored; for to the people at large, educated as well as simple, they must always be the outward sign of what is within: the nations of the earth judge a Church by what it looks like—by its external fruits in worship and in works—not by what little conclaves of cultivated theologians say that it is; and hence it comes that widespread and deep-rooted religious controversies fix themselves on external things, as in the Iconoclastic controversy of one age or the Vestiarian of another. The former controversy happened eleven centuries ago; but its effects have been profound and ineffaceable because, being external, they touched every soldier and statesman, every washerwoman and peasant in Christendom. So it will always be. If the

Anglican Church wishes to be considered merely Protestant by the world she must look merely Protestant ; if imitation-Roman, she must look imitation-Roman (she can never be mistaken for a really Romanist Church) ; if Catholic and Evangelical, she must look Catholic and Evangelical—and this is just what the Ornaments Rubric enables her to do.

She must justify her faith to the people, she must plainly show her real character to the nations. That real character is precisely what the modern world needs —a religion that has the freedom, depth, simplicity of the New Testament, the exquisite fervour and mystery of devotion which was developed in the Primitive Church, the peculiar beauty of worship which underlies all the accretions of centuries, and shines out resplendent when these are stripped away—as they are by the Ornaments Rubric. Can anything else finally satisfy the craving for religion which grows around us from day to day ? Certainly not the ill-attended services, the unloved, formalist indifferentism, which has long blighted the historic Protestant Churches, as travellers in Holland, Germany, and Switzerland know too well ; nor the effeminacy which has overspread Romanist worship, especially in the Latin countries ; but Catholicism, freed from the tyrannies and trivialities which have grown up round it. Catholicism reformed, in fact, is what will meet the needs of the thoughtful and devout who are asking for bread. And this is what the English Church can give. It is her influence—if she will be true to herself—that can gradually transform Christendom. For either the Roman Catholic Church must reform herself to a free and purified Catholicism, or she will continue to sink, with that appalling rapidity which recent statistics have brought before us ; and either Protestantism must move towards this Evangelical Catholicism (as in many ways it is already doing), or it will drift along the other line of its development and lose its creed altogether.

Perhaps I may be allowed to illustrate what I believe to be true in the realm of ceremonial—the great art of public worship—by some words recently spoken by the Bishop of Oxford in another connection: [1]

"I suppose that the real reason why we desire Church Reform is because we believe in the special mission or vocation of that part of Christendom which we call the Church of England. And, certainly, as I look around and think of things as they are now, and compare them with things as they were thirty or forty years ago, I feel this distinctive mission of the Church of England more, and not less—incomparably more. I mean that during that period we have witnessed a perpetual growth in what I may call the Romanization of the Roman Catholic Communion, and a constant process on the other side of disintegration of the old doctrinal standards and appeals of Protestantism, without any apparent ability to restore the foundations that are being weakened. So that, if you look to the right or to the left, it seems to me that everything that happens in the course of recent years increases and does not diminish our sense of that special vocation, mission, and opportunity which belong to the Church of England. I will very briefly seek to define it. It stands upon the ancient Creeds which represent the witness of the Christian Church to facts from the beginning, and the primeval aboriginal beliefs of the Church about God, and about Christ, and about man. It stands on that ancient foundation which, if anything in the world is to be called Catholic, is Catholic: and, side by side with that, it in the sixteenth century recalled —I do not say adopted, but recalled—the great principle which is the principle of ecclesiastical liberty at the bottom, I mean the appeal to Scripture; for wherever that appeal is candidly and clearly applied as a matter of principle, it prevents that which goes on, and always must go on, where that appeal is suppressed—the constant accretion of dogmas and the constant restriction, therefore, of the field of liberty of opinion. Where the appeal to Scripture is

[1] Speech in the Church House, Westminster, by Dr. Gore, then Bishop of Birmingham, at the Annual Meeting of the Church Reform League, May 26, 1911. From the *Quarterly Chronicle* of the Church Reform League, London, 1911, vol. vi, no. 7, p. 197.

required and is made real for anything to be part of the
faith of the Church, there you have a constant restriction
of this power of the Church in the accretion of dogmas
and doctrine. You have the field of liberty constantly
kept open. Then the Church of England stands upon
the Episcopate as the ancient principle both of continuity
and of cohesion, and upon the administration of the Sacra-
ments as they have been in the Christian Church from
the beginning. That is all very familiar; but it does give
our Communion an altogether distinctive position as you
look about in the forces of Christendom, and my belief in
the quite infinite value of that distinctive position, in view
of all that has been going on outside the Church of England, in the Church of Rome, and in Nonconformist
bodies, grows and strengthens from year to year. Yet
I do not think anything is more certain than that as a
body we are not making the best of our case—that as a
body we are not doing what we have every opportunity of
doing: that is, making ourselves and what we stand for
intelligible. The world does not know—to a very large
extent we do not know ourselves—what we stand for,
because we will not trouble our heads about principles,
because we do almost anything in the world sooner than
think, and for that reason we cannot make ourselves
intelligible; we cannot make the best of that plainly
divine vocation and opportunity which belongs to us."

Let the Church of England, then, show herself to the
world for what she is. Let her raise the banner of a pure
Catholicism. Now that banner, that evident oriflamme,
must be her public worship.

She has not done so in the past; and to this is due her
partial failure. But she is alive, vigorous, hopeful, and in
the future she can be what she has as yet failed to be.

The lawlessness of the present age is known to all men.
Its record is written out in that multitudinous dreary
collection which is called the Report of the Royal Commission on Ecclesiastical Discipline. Few, indeed, of the
services there described could be for a moment defended

before any impartial 'tribunal. The result has been a general depreciation of the public estimate of clerical honour. But what people fail to realize is that this "disloyalty" was no new thing: it was equally characteristic of the eighteenth and seventeenth centuries, not to mention the sixteenth. Let me therefore quote at length from what are perhaps the most valuable and interesting pages of that vast collection—the notes of the Bishop of Gloucester, describing the liberties taken with the Book of Common Prayer since the enactment of the last Act of Uniformity. It is important that these facts should be widely known. '

Dr. Gibson here deals with the period after the last revision of the Prayer Book and the passing of the Act of Uniformity of 1662. This third attempt to enforce conformity ended disastrously in a further schism and the ejection of a large number of ministers: yet, Dr. Gibson shows, it was found impossible to insist on strict observance of the law; many irregularities speedily crept in, and were generally tolerated:

"(1) *Omissions to Comply with the Requirements of the Rubrics.*

"(a) *In spite of the ornaments rubric and the 24th Canon, there is no evidence that copes were generally worn in Cathedrals and Collegiate Churches.*—Indeed the only places in which it can be shown that they were used are Norwich, Westminster, and Durham. At *Norwich* one was given at the Restoration by Philip Harbord, the High Sheriff of Norfolk (see Blomefield's *Topographical History of Norfolk,* iv. 6). At *Westminster,* Thoresby was scandalized by the sight of the exceedingly rich copes and robes in 1680 (*Diary,* i. 60, 61); but they were apparently only used on occasions of exceptional ceremony, as Coronations. At *Durham* they were seen in 1681 by Thoresby, who was 'amazed at their . . . rich embroidered copes, vestments, etc.' (*Diary,* i. 75); and they continued to be habitually used till 1759, when, 'at the latter end of July, or beginning of August, the old copes

---

' Royal Commission on Ecclesiastical Discipline. *Appendices, Index, and Analysis of Evidence,* vol. iv, pp. 54–56. London, 1906. Wyman, Fetter Lane, E.C.

(those rags of Popery), which had been used at the Communion service of the Abbey ever since the time of the Reformation, were ordered by the Dean and Chapter to be totally disused and laid aside. Dr. Warburton, one of the Prebendaries and Bishop of Gloucester, was very zealous to have them laid aside, and so was Dr. Cowper, the Dean' (Gyll's *Diary*, quoted in the notes to *Cosin's Correspondence*, vol. i, p. 170).

" (*b*) *Even the surplice was not always worn in Parish Churches.* — The clergyman of Little Gransden, before Barnabas Oley, 'never wore the surplice, except on Communion Days, and that was but twice a year' (Overton's *Life in the English Church*, p. 189). Dean Granville (1684) complains that his curate at Kilkhampton, in order 'to please the dow-baked people of that country, used to officiate without a surplice' (Granville's *Letters*, etc., ii. 158). Bishop Croft of Hereford wrote in 1675, 'to be zealous for the surplice is not wise'; and, according to Mr. Overton, 'at the end of the seventeenth century many Low Church clergy were wont so far to violate the Act of Uniformity as often not to wear the surplice at all in church.' They would 'sometimes wear it,' said South, in a sermon preached in King William III's reign (*Sermons*, iv. 191), and 'oftener lay it aside' (*The English Church in the Eighteenth Century*, ii. p. 469).

" (*c*) *The rubric requiring weekly Communion, ' at the least' in Cathedrals and Collegiate Churches was scandalously neglected.* — In 1681 Dean Comber speaks as if 'monthly Communions' were all that were generally to be found in cathedrals; and Dean Granville's *Correspondence* of the same period bears witness to the neglect in many places. About 1680 he says that the rubric was not observed in more than two cathedrals, and two or three chapels in all England (*Letters*, ii. 45). Granville himself was indefatigable in his endeavours to restore the weekly celebration at Durham, and elsewhere, and had a certain measure of success, but it was certainly not the custom at York, or Rochester or Windsor in 1684 (see Granville's *Letters*, etc., ii. p. 85 *seq.*, 125, etc.). In far later times there was also much neglect, e.g. the weekly celebration of Holy Communion was not begun in Wells Cathedral till 1872, and there were no Saints' day celebrations, till after 1882.

"(*d*) *An extraordinary number of irregularities were toler-ated in the service.*—Striking evidence of this is given by a letter from a student in the Inns of Courts, written to Dean Granville about 1680. The writer set himself to try to 'find an entire service performed exactly according to the rubric, without any exercise of the prudence of a private man,' but had to confess that he was unable to discover one such 'in all London.'

"'We have,' says he, 'as many separate ways of worship as we have ministers, and every one that I could yet discover offends in something that is clearly contrary to law. . . . One cuts off the preparatory exhortation, *Dearly beloved brethren, etc.* Another the *Benedictus* and *Jubilate*, and satisfieth himself with a Psalm in metre instead thereof, out of Sternhold and Hopkins. . . . A third brings in part of the Visitation Office, commanded to be said in the sick man's presence, into the public congregation. . . . A fourth adds very formally a preface of his own to the recital of the creed, though he would not allow of one of the Church's to the whole service. A fifth jumbles both first and second service together, cutting off not only the concluding prayer of St. Chrysostom, and the *Grace of our Lord Jesus Christ*, but also our Lord's Prayer in the front of the Communion Office, which I have always looked on as an extraordinary piece of boldness. A sixth, more presumptuously, not only cuts off the Lord's Prayer alone, but both the Lord's Prayer and Nicene Creed also. A seventh, who avoids these irregularities, yet presumes after sermon to cut off the Prayer for the Church Militant, and the final Benediction, *The peace of God, etc.*, hoping to satisfy his congregation (but I am sure he never satisfied me) with a benediction of his own choice, and prayer of his own composure. An eighth jostles out the Office of Churching or public thanksgiving of women after childbirth till after the Benediction and departure of the congregation. . . . A ninth takes as great liberty with the Sacrament of Baptism as others do with

the ordinary service, and will not allow it the honour the
Church designs, in being done after the Second Lesson in
the face of a congregation . . . shuffling it over, as I have
often seen at a font, sometimes unhappily placed in a corner,
with not above ten persons to assist thereat. . . . A tenth
on a Sacrament day takes upon him, contrary to the design
of the Church, gravely to dismiss his congregation with
a blessing for profanely turning their backs upon God's
altar, pronouncing the very *Peace of God* to those that pro-
claim a manifest contempt of their Saviour's death and
passion, by a sinful departure when they are invited to
that heavenly feast. . . . Sir, if I should prosecute the
clergy in this point of their irregularities, I should make
my letter like a fanatic sermon, and come up to one and
thirteenthly, which would tire both you and me also   The
other things therefore at present I shall only hint to you in
gross, namely the reading of the Communion Service in
the desk, when the Church appoints it at the altar.   The
reading no service at all in most churches weekly, when
the Church commands it to be in every one daily.   Catechizing the children but only in Lent, when the Church
commands it throughout the whole year; and when they
do catechize, performing that duty on week days, in a very
small assembly, when the Church commands it to be done
on Sundays and Holydays in the afternoon, and when here
in our city we may assure ourselves of a very full congregation.   Churching women in the chamber, as well as
visiting the sick in the church.   Baptizing children almost
generally in private houses, without the least appearance
of necessity · and administering the Communion . . . also
oftentimes to the whole in private, where they have no
conveniency of a chapel. . . . And these three last duties
most commonly performed, as our burials are, without
the surplice, and sometimes, I have seen, without a gown'
(see *Dean Granville's Letters*, etc., ii. 101 *seq.*).

"Besides these thus generally noted, the following irregularities deserve more particular mention :

"(*e*) *Communicants receiving either standing or sitting* —In
the life of Bishop Frampton (1680-1691) an account is given

of a clergyman who 'for thirty years was not able to prove
he had once in that time received the Sacrament of the
Lord's Supper ; for his manner was after Consecration to
carry the holy elements into the reading desk, and then
return, and in a most uncanonical manner distribute them
to the parishioners,' (Evans' *Life of Frampton*, p. 139).
According to Hickes the Nonjuror, Archbishop Tillotson
(1691–1694) was 'accustomed to administer the Lord's
Supper to some persons sitting,' and 'walked round the
chapel (at Lincoln's Inn) administering the elements, first
to those who were seated in their pews, and then to those
who were kneeling at the rails' (see Lathbury's *History
of the Nonjurors*, p. 156). Nor was this a solitary case.
The Bishop of St. Asaph, Hickes mentions, adopted the
same practice ; and Croft, Bishop of Hereford (1675),
actually advised the clergy to dispense with the rule that
required kneeling (see Overton's *Life in the English Church*,
p. 171).

"(*f*) *Omissions in the service.*— South, in one of his
sermons, speaks of the Divine Service as 'so curtailed as
if the people were to have but the tenths of it from the
priests' (*Sermons*, iv. 191). Early in the 18th century some
of the Arian clergy actually missed out the second and
third petitions in the Litany and altered the doxology
(Whiston's *Memoirs*) ; and the Athanasian Creed was 'quite
as often omitted in the 18th century as our own,' its
use being forbidden in the King's Chapel in George III's
time (see Abbey and Overton, *The English Church in the
Eighteenth Century*, vol. ii, p. 476).

"(*g*) *The use of 'pulpit prayers,'* i.e. long extempore
prayers interpolated before the sermon 'sometimes longer
than the whole service.'—This was a common practice,
against which the stricter churchmen strongly protested,
but it was frequently adopted by the Puritans. Thus South
speaks of 'those long prayers so frequently used by some
before the sermons,' and calls them 'new serious prayers in
the pulpit' (*Sermons*, vol. i, p. 353). See also Dean Granville's
Letters, vol. ii, pp. 104, 111, 112, where he speaks strongly
on the 'notorious irregularity of preachers, even in the

King's Chapel, in using a prayer before the sermon, and sometimes a very long one.'

"(h) *Neglect of the observance of ' Litany days' (Wednesday and Friday), of Saints' days, and even of Good Friday and Ascension Day.*—See Abbey and Overton, *English Church in the Eighteenth Century,* ii. 446–50 ; and cf. Bishop Butler's *Durham Charge* (1751): 'A great part of this [the external forms of religion] is neglected by the generality amongst us ; for instance, the services of the church, not only upon common days, but also upon Saints' days '"

On the other hand, Bishop Gibson goes on to note, "in spite of growing carelessness, instances still occur of ceremonial usages and ornaments not prescribed in the Book of Common Prayer"[1]; and he mentions—the mixed chalice, unleavened bread, altar lights, bowing towards the altar on entering and leaving church, and the cross as an ornament.[2]

The moral which Dr. Gibson draws is that conformity cannot be enforced by law. That we have long known if the lawyers have not. And it is good that it should be pressed, good that impassive lawyers and hysterical members of Parliament should alike have it urged upon them by the bishop's learning. We may or may not agree with another bishop who once declared that he would rather see England free than England sober ; but we should all, I think, agree that we would rather see England free in religion than orthodox by compulsion—driven by a system of fines to attend a service at which the rubrics (always

[1] "Not prescribed in the Book of Common Prayer" is the Bishop's own phrase We might demur to the use of words which seem to suggest unlawfulness in the customs mentioned, and which in themselves are scarcely accurate , for, not only have the mixed chalice and altar lights been declared lawful, but altar lights and the cross, having been in lawful use in the second year of King Edward VI, are prescribed in the Book of Common Prayer, and unleavened bread is still covered by the rubric, though ordinary bread is allowed to suffice Bowing is a custom the lawfulness of which has never, we believe, been seriously called in question

[2] For much information as to post-Reformation ceremonial usages see Vernon Staley, *Hierurgia Anglicana,* new edition, 3 vols , London, A Moring, 1902; and cf , for evidence as to more loyal observance of Prayer Book in the eighteenth century, J Wickham Legg, *London Church Services in and about the Reign of Queen Anne* in the Transactions of the St Paul's Ecclesiological Society, Vol. II, Part I   London, Harrison & Sons, 1906

excepting the Ornaments Rubric) were carried out by
clergy trembling under the rod of deprivation.

You cannot enforce a system of worship. Even the
iron-bound system of Rome has failed here. Since she
has attempted to dictate uniformity, she has found herself
obliged to follow the last popular fashion, however puerile
and however effeminate, far more than in the comparative freedom of the middle ages. The learned Roman
Catholic liturgiologist Mr. Edmund Bishop has well stated
this fact: [1]

"With the missal and breviary of S. Pius V, the
Pontifical of Gregory XIII, the Ritual of Paul V, and,
finally, the Cæremoniale Episcoporum of Urban VIII, the
history of the Roman liturgy may be said to be closed;
there have indeed been alterations and revisions since, but
the changes made have been comparatively unimportant.

"From the fact that the issue of these Roman service
books of the sixteenth and seventeenth centuries, with
their adoption by all the [Roman Catholic] churches of
the West, closes, and doubtless finally closes, that chapter
of liturgical history, it must not be inferred that the
different racial tendencies of mind and spirit, which
exhibited themselves in the Roman or Gothic and Gallican
missals of the sixth or seventh or eighth centuries, and
are so clearly evidenced in the modifications to which the
Roman rite was subjected in the later middle ages, were
no longer active nor seeking to assert themselves in public
worship in our churches; but that spirit has gone another
way to work. In the middle ages that effusive, affective,
and devotional spirit continually made itself felt in modifications in the liturgical books themselves, and in the mode
of carrying out the strictly official or liturgical public
services. This explains the great variety and diversity of
the rituals, missals, and breviaries of later medieval times;
and it explains also how the books of devotion of those
days, contrary to what is common now, were drawn up

[1] Edmund Bishop, *The Genius of the Roman Rite*. Reprinted in *Essays on Ceremonial*, ed. Vernon Staley. London: 1904, A. Moring, "The Library of Liturgiology and Ecclesiology," vol. iv, pp. 305-07.

on the lines of the official service books themselves ; or,
as some people have put it, 'there were no popular devotions in those days ' But this was only because the popular
devotional spirit expressed itself with freedom and liberty in
the strictly liturgical services of the various local churches

"By the action of S. Pius V, and his successors, in
stamping the Roman books put forth by them with a
definite character, and by the institution of a Congregation of Rites designed to keep observances on the lines
laid down in those books, such manipulation of the public
service books of the Church as was common in the middle
ages in every country in Europe, was destined to be finally
put an end to.   But the spirit then active has never ceased
to be active still, and it still finds a field for its operations.
Unable to act inside and on the liturgy itself, it acts with
yet greater freedom without.   One path shut up, it seeks
its ends by another.   And this is the explanation of the
rapid growth, the wonderful variety, and great development in the last two or three centuries, of what we call,
to distinguish them from the fixed official services, 'devotions'; whilst they are evidence, too, that the two spirits
betraying themselves so clearly in the first mass-books of
which we have knowledge, exist in their duality still."

You cannot enforce a system of worship.   Nor can
even the Papal autocracy prevent the introduction of extra
services.

What, then, can you do?   Just what is done in literature, in art, in science, in politics, in every branch of
human activity.   You can educate.   You can search out
the facts, you can spread knowledge, you can establish
principles.   You can show men the beauty of the right
way.   You can also remove the remnants of autocratic
ignorance which still unhappily linger among some of our
bishops, or at least you can secure that the young men
who are now learning shall know and understand when
some of them come to such positions of authority ; and
you can spread the spirit of loyalty among clergy and lay-
folk alike, if only on this ground—that the spirit of individualism has proved a failure.

It is to foster such knowledge and such a spirit that the Alcuin Club exists, resting upon no party, but appealing to the scientific spirit and the love of noble art, and basing all its work upon "strict obedience" to the Prayer Book.

Antinomy has been tried, and has failed in every form. Every man has done what was right in his own eyes, with the result that every man has done wrong. This was disastrous; but if every man will now be content to learn, to think, and to carry out his appointed duty, if every priest will use the great opportunity which the Prayer Book offers, and if every bishop—true to that "sound learning" which Bishop Creighton described as the key-note of our part of the Church Catholic, and which is as necessary in public worship as in public speech—if every bishop will wisely lead, using the crook of a shepherd, and not the driver's whip which disperses and does not direct, then we may in the future be true to ourselves, and of service to a world which is much distracted by the follies of Christians and their moral failures.

The Anglican Church has partly failed, in that she has missed great opportunities, has allowed her place to be taken over large areas by vigorous Nonconformist bodies, has suffered vast masses to lapse into indifference. And this has largely been because her sons have not been loyal, have not carried out her system. They have never given it a chance. We appeal to them now to give it that chance, to try the experiment which ought to have been tried centuries ago. If the Prayer Book rules about teaching alone had been loyally obeyed by our forefathers, we could not have lost our people as we have. So it is with other matters.[1]

I will not dwell upon them here except to remark that the degradation of the Anglican services had produced in the days of our fathers a system of worship that was not only doleful and repulsive but also profoundly unspiritual;

---

[1] I have tried to explain this in two pamphlets, *The Training of a Christian according to the Prayer Book and Canons*, and *Loyalty to the Prayer Book*, both published by Mowbrays.

and that, although we have very largely replaced what was doleful by what is called "bright," we have not yet restored the thrill and joy, the love and wonder, the fervour and mystery, the atmosphere of Divine presence, which are the characteristics of true worship. On our holidays, perhaps, we go into the church nearest where we happen to be: and we find a cold formality, the lifeless and loveless performance of a service more or less mutilated, which entirely fails to justify its supposed purpose—the worship of God. We might sometimes almost cry within our hearts—

> "Great God! I'd rather be
> A pagan suckled in a creed outworn;
> So might I, standing on this pleasant lea,
> Have glimpses that would make me less forlorn."

A Salvation Army service (we may sometimes say to ourselves after a particularly exasperating experience), a gathering of Primitive Methodists, a silent meeting of Quakers, or a low Mass in some chapel abroad—all these would have some fervour, some meaning to the worshippers, some little care, some little glow of affection. But this grinding out of a routine, dreary from its heartless reading and horrid music, this dull amalgam of Mattins, Litany, Ante-Communion, and perfunctory sermon—this heavy foundation without a temple, this stale effort without a point—where is there worship to be found here? Why (we may even have been tempted to say) should we come here at all? Why not say our Mattins, Litany, and even the Ante-Communion, quietly and reverently together in the garden of the house where we are staying, or in the chapel? We shall miss nothing except the sermon, the quest for alms, and the despairing sentimentality of a few hymns from a nineteenth-century collection!

Many do stay away. This is anti-social; but there is sometimes much temptation. Also, in the towns, every now and then some one joins the Church of Rome, which people do, not because they yearn for any Italian autocracy, but because they find no food for their souls in their parish church, and do genuinely long for worship.

Of course multitudes of our churches have climbed out
of this slough of despond, while often it is the congregations
(because they have been untaught) who keep the clergy to
the old routine which the congregations are used to sitting
out before dinner. But, alas! how common this type of
service still is! How one dreads to find this sort of church,
and how very often one does find it!

Now it is this misery of formalism—unblamed by the
authorities—which has been the real weakness of our
Church—just as it is the Prayer Book, so far as it has been
carried out, which has always been its strength. Unless
such formalism passes speedily away, it will be a greater
weakness in the near future; for people no longer go to
church as an unpleasant duty which it is not respectable
to omit. The present generation increasingly goes where
it likes going, and otherwise does not go, but enjoys the
sky or the fireside. The old-fashioned congregation, still
powerful to grumble, is dwindling day by day. The newer
generation must have love, joy, peace, beauty, and praise,
and worship. People are becoming very detached in their
notions of religious allegiance; they will go where they
get help, where they find the spirit of prayer—for the
unspiritual will not now go much to church from duty
or convention, as they did in the past.

The hungry sheep, who so often are not fed, the wander-
ing sheep, who so often are not led, do not require or desire
anything very elaborate. In many ways we have had too
much elaboration of the wrong kind, and but little building-
up of true worship—much embroidery upon sorry stuff, and
more lace than clothing. We have now to turn to the
essential things, as many of the clergy are already doing;
and, laying aside mere party cries and badges, and theological narrownesses and prejudices, to join together in the
fervour of worship and the beauty of holiness. The historic
worship of Christendom never lost that talent of devotion,
and the English Church expressly bade her sons retain it
when she ordained that the old ways were to prevail in
their purity.

All that Christian men need and want the Anglican

Churches can give them. The Prayer Book as it stands provides four short services for each Sunday, which, loyally carried out, are a joy and delight to every worshipper.¹ Why not try them? One of them, and that the chief, is pictured and described in the pages which follow.

---

¹ These short services are called Mattins, Litany, Holy Communion, and Evensong The law also requires a sermon in the morning, and catechizing in the afternoon or evening, and allows hymns, which may be very beautiful, some of which are occasionally sung in procession

A 'LOW-CHURCH' CELEBRATION

INTRODUCTORY PICTURE

I HAVE called this Plate by the unscientific title of "A 'low-church' Celebration," in order to draw attention sharply to the fact that party divisions on ceremonial matters ought not to exist, and have no logical right to existence. There is, in the light of present knowledge, little to dispute about: and therefore a most serious responsibility rests on those who remain disputatious.

Those who like a "low-church" or extremely plain type of service will, I hope, feel that this picture meets their needs; and at the same time it will be a real satisfaction to them to know that the standard here shown would satisfy the most exacting ritualist. Here then is a point of unity: the rest is a matter of taste or of opportunity, not a matter for quarrel.

There is no need, then, to revise the Ornaments Rubric.

The plain service here figured satisfies it to the letter   The
village parson of Evangelical views is here shown as entirely
loyal to the Rubric,—Why, then, alter it by making it elastic
and illogical ? He has a strong objection to what some of his
friends call Popish mass-vestments , but he knows that the
Popish chasuble [1] is but a degraded form of St Paul's great-
coat, and he feels that in wearing the garment which is now
agreed to be the cloke or *phelones* [2] which St. Paul left at
Troas, he is protesting in the happiest way for the purity of
Pauline doctrine against subsequent degradations of it

This additional picture will also, I hope, guard the reader
at the outset against the impression that an elaborate ceremonial is thought desirable for ordinary churches.   The
parson of an average parish will probably be in wisdom
content with something between the very plain and the
very ornate, while even those churches which use a rich
ceremonial will, we may venture to hope, maintain a
wholesome simplicity of action

[1] I confess to a momentary feeling of despair when I discovered that the
editors of the admirable *Concise Oxford Dictionary* define *Chasuble* as "Short
back and breast vestment of celebrant at Mass or Eucharist " We can hardly
blame Churchmen for ignorance, when the best small dictionary in existence
describes the chasuble as if it looked like a chest-protector

[2] 2 Tim iv 13   See Convocation of Canterbury, Upper House, *The
Ornaments of the Church and its Ministers*, p 10, n 8 (1908, No. 416, London,
S P C K).   The *phelones* (I atinized as *pænula*) became the *phelonion*, as the
garment is still called in the East   The late Latin *casula* (chasuble) is merely
a kind of nick-name, meaning a little hut or tent (casubula), because it covered
the wearer so completely   Cf. p 48, n 1

PREFACE

WITH ESPECIAL REFERENCE TO THE ENGLISH AND AMERICAN USES

WRITTEN explanations are difficult to understand and slow to convince, compared with those means which appeal more directly to the eye. The Committee of the Alcuin Club has therefore ventured on the experiment of publishing a series of twelve drawings to illustrate the service of the Holy Eucharist in the Anglican Communion at the present day, following thus on the series of miniatures which the club has already reproduced from the fifteenth-century French *Exposition de la Messe*, and on the woodcuts which it has reprinted from the sixteenth-century Flemish *Dat Boexken vander Missen*.

The Committee has found in Mr. C. O. Skilbeck an artist who thoroughly understands the worship and history of the English Church, and who himself attends a church where the rubrics of the Prayer Book, and the customs and canons which those rubrics illustrate, are conscientiously carried out. He has thus been able accurately to draw actual scenes from the service at which he is constantly present, and to avoid the dangers which arise from attempts to reproduce imaginary happenings. At the same time he has, for the sake of clearness and intelligibility, made the pictures diagrammatic; and he has also varied the design of the altar and vestments, in the hope that the illustrations might in this way be of rather more assistance to architects and to those other craftsmen and craftswomen who are concerned in the furniture and decoration of our churches. For the sake of clearness he has designedly left his architecture sketchy in character, and has not substituted reredoses for dorsals.[1] This can, of course, be done in any church, so long as the reredos is planned on the same lines as the dorsal, and is of about the same size; but the elaborate tabernacle work of a good reredos does not lend itself to diagrammatic illustration: nor could an adequate idea of its beauty be given in a black-and-white drawing; and the Committee would shrink from suggesting, even to the most casual observer, that it regards as tolerable the nineteenth-century fashion of making carved reredoses without colour and gilding.

THE ENGLISH USE

The Communion service here illustrated is that of the English Use, "the use," as the title-page of, the Prayer Book says "of the Church of England," which is that which obtains over the greater part of the whole Anglican Church. The American Church, which also forms part of the Anglican Communion, has a use of its own, which will be described later: so has the Irish Church, although in this case the use is of a peculiarly restricted character, owing to the absence of an Ornaments Rubric and the presence of certain special canons, so that these pictures cannot serve to illustrate it. The Scottish Episcopal Church has a liturgy of its own, upon which the American Liturgy was based.

It is so obvious that the English Use is the use of the Church of England that we need not, in the year 1911, waste any words in proving this over again. No one now ventures openly to defend the Romanizing position in print, not even in the chartered licence of the correspondence columns of Church newspapers. "Roman" details are indeed still not uncommon in some churches, since men cling to accustomed things, and those who have grown old in a bad habit do not usually alter; but the disappearance of our nineteenth-century mistakes is only a matter of time. Logic, conscience, learning, will do their work, and are doing it, so that loyalty and loveliness increase every year.

[1] An example of a reredos is therefore given in the frontispiece.

THE AMERICAN USE

This is the position in England and in those churches of our Communion which use our Prayer Book. In America, however, the case is different. The American Church, unfortunately, discarded the Ornaments Rubric; and the result has been that the decadent ceremonial of modern Rome has rooted itself rather deeply in the Protestant Episcopal Church of the United States. This evil has been assisted by the comparative absence of tradition in a new country, by the comparative dearth of beautiful things, such as pictures, and old churches and homesteads, and also by the paucity of liturgical scholars in the States. There are signs of awakening now, the breath of better things; but until recently the "advanced" churches openly followed the Baltimore Roman Catholic Directory, while other churches were often tinged with their example.[1]

American Churchmen are awakening. They ask now, "What should be our right principle in ceremonial matters?" Hitherto most of their "advanced" men have answered, "As we have no Ornaments Rubric, we should follow the Western Use."

Now that is an answer which liturgical study rapidly dissolves. Let me apply the solvent in the words of Mr. F. C. Eeles:

"MODERN WESTERN" USE

"A very misleading use has been made of the word *Western* by some English Churchmen. They have applied the word to Roman ritual or Roman ceremonial, when they have desired to avoid using the word 'Roman.' It has been assumed that the Roman rite and Roman ceremonial have become so universal in the West (except only in this country) that the terms 'Roman' and 'Western' are interchangeable. Even if this were the case, it would be absurd to use the word in this way, inasmuch as there

[1] Romanizing directions were published by Messrs. McGarvey and Burnett, whom an awakening of the logical instinct caused afterwards to join the Roman Catholic Church.

E

would still be two Western uses at least, the English Prayer Book being one of them—i.e of course, if the Church in these 'Western' islands of Great Britain and Ireland be a part of the Catholic Church. At the very least this use of the word 'Western' for 'Roman' would suggest the utter illegitimacy of everything done in this country. But even if we confine the term 'Western' to the rest of the Western churches—the churches, that is to say, of the Papal obedience—we find that it is untrue to facts to use the term 'Western' for 'Roman,' however helpful such a use may be in commending modern Italian customs to ignorant and unsuspecting people who are unwilling to do what they believe to be Roman.

"In the first place, what are the facts?

"Besides the Roman rite several other rites are still used in the West (as well, of course, as our own). The Ambrosian is used throughout the diocese of Milan and even beyond it, serving over a million souls In the diocese of Lyons, the Lyons rite is used. In two places in Spain the Mozarabic rite is used. In Portugal the old rite of Braga survives in one place at least. The older religious orders still use their own rites — the Carthusian, Dominican, and Cistercian. All these have a perfect right to be called Western uses.

"Then as regards ceremonial. There are not only the ceremonial variations which accompany these different rites which we have specified, but there are more. In Spain, although the text of the service books is now Roman, the old Spanish ceremonial still remains to a very large extent. Like Dominican and Carthusian customs, and much that is done at Milan, this Spanish ceremonial is Gallican in character, and very much like the Old English ; but it is 'modern Western use' for all that. At Venice local uses remain; in Germany; in Austria; in certain French churches; even in Belgium. Indeed, to find the Roman ceremonial which Anglican Romanizers have delighted to copy, one must look to the churches of Jesuits, Oratorians, or Redemptorists ; to certain new French churches ; to parish churches in Rome and some other Italian towns; and above all to Roman Catholic churches in England and America.

"Indeed, there are two kinds of Roman ceremonial, for there is not only the popular Roman use of the class of church just mentioned, but the more strictly Roman use of the great basilicas, whose practice would by no means satisfy some of our friends. A story is told of a Roman Catholic from the Continent who went into a certain English church where the rector claimed that he was following Roman use. 'Well,' said the Roman Catholic, 'why do you pile up all that vulgar stuff behind the high altar? There is nothing of the kind on the high altar of St. Peter's at Rome.' The only answer the rector could make was, 'You cannot expect poor little St. X——'s to be like the chief church of Christendom.'

"Lastly, what is the history of the extensive prevalence of the Roman books on the Continent at the present day? How did this state of things come about? Is it a case of the survival of the fittest? By no means, although this is often said to be the case. It is entirely through the ultramontane and uncatholic policy of the Roman court in quite recent times. It was Pius IX who destroyed the French diocesan uses. The Roman missal and breviary were not used in the parish churches of France until quite recently: there are plenty of people still living who remember the French diocesan service books. Has the Church of France been healthier or happier since she fell under the spell of ultramontanism? Is her theological learning of world-wide renown now, as it was in the days of the great Gallican bishops of the seventeenth and early eighteenth centuries, who were active in reforming and maintaining their diocesan rites and ceremonies? The question is absurd: nearly all individuality has been crushed out of the French Church, and the national feeling, once so proud of its Gallican 'liberties' and traditions, now finds an illegitimate outlet in attacking the Christianity which has denied it all legitimate means of expression."

What, then, is the right principle for American Churchmen? Let us suppose that their Church were to decide to use henceforth the service books of the Russian Church. If they took over the Russian ritual, is there any doubt as to what ceremonial they would use with it ? They would certainly not use a garbled form of Roman ceremonial ; they would carry out Russian services with their proper Russian adjuncts.

So it is with them now, *ceteris paribus* They have not made up a new ritual ; therefore they are not called upon to make up a new ceremonial. They have not taken over the Greek ritual, nor the Roman ritual ; and therefore they cannot logically use the Greek ceremonial nor the Roman ceremonial. But they have taken over, with but slight changes, the English and Scottish ritual, and therefore every principle and precedent, every consideration of logic and consistency requires them to carry out this ritual with the ceremonial that belongs to it. They have not an Ornaments Rubric, unfortunately for them ; they share this calamity with the Irish Church : the sooner they settle such matters by canon, or by a revision, the better (if the time is ripe for sound decisions) ; but, in the meantime, their course is clear—they can carry out their services, which are Anglican, in the Anglican manner They are not in the undignified position of being without any standard, and having to borrow plumes from another Communion which is most regretably hostile, and scorns them when they stultify their own position by mimetic methods. One might perhaps borrow from a Church with which one is in communion, without loss of self-respect, but to imitate (and that without permission and without any possibility of successful imitation) a Church which denies one's very existence, is to forfeit not self-respect only but the respect also of others.

All this is so plain, simple, and irrefutable, that we need have little fear as to the ultimate triumph of the new school of American ritualists. Only we in England must help them by being true to ourselves, and by holding closer intercourse with them in the future, both for our own advantage and for theirs The Alcuin Club, for example, should spread in America as much as in England.

We therefore give below a general survey, a brief ceremonial directory, for the American Church, as well as one
for the English Church.

The service illustrated in these twelve pictures is that
of the Sunday Eucharist with full ceremonial, and full
complement of ministers. It is always of more practical
utility to illustrate such matters in their fullest form, because
every one can omit what is impossible or undesirable in his
own case—as, for instance, it is impossible in many places
to have three ministers and undesirable to have incense.

But it is an error to suppose that there is any reason
why a hard and fast distinction should be drawn between
a "High" and a "Low" celebration of the Holy Eucharist.
A service in which the celebrant is assisted by gospeller
and epistoler, or, to use other words, deacon and subdeacon,
is the *norm* of the Eucharistic service. Celebrations without
these assistant ministers are makeshifts at best, allowed by
the Church as a concession to circumstances.

Now, many people think that the deacon and subdeacon
are a sort of enrichment, suitable for a "ritualistic"
church, and that they ought only to be present when every
possible scrap of elaborate ceremonial can be carried out.
It would be difficult to make a greater mistake. That
sharp distinction now made by our Roman Catholic
brethren between High and Low Mass is a modern
innovation contrary to the general practice of the whole
Church. It has produced the service known as *Missa
Cantata*, viz. a Low Mass sung by a single priest assisted
only by servers. At this form of service the use of incense
has been forbidden in recent times by the Roman Congregation of Rites; and, on the other hand, a High Mass
cannot now take place without incense, according to
strict Roman usage. Both prohibitions, however, are very
modern. Some years ago they were copied by a few
Anglicans, who, by having a "Missa Cantata" on modern
Roman lines, tried (with a heroism out of proportion to
their sense of humour) to keep within Roman rules and

yet to obey Dr. Temple's Lambeth "Opinion" at one and the same time.

Until the destruction of the national French rites by Pope Pius IX, a High Mass, without portable lights or incense and with very little ceremonial, was quite common all over France, as it has been throughout the West from the very earliest times   Indeed, such a service may still be seen on ferial days in the diocese of Lyons, which even now retains much of the old Lyons Use; and services of this description must have been very common in this country also. We would earnestly plead for such a form of simple High Mass now, wherever the fuller ceremonial is impossible.   Far be it from us to deprecate the use of incense and movable lights, which we believe to be lawful in the Church of England. But there are many places where this full ceremonial can-not be used ; indeed, in the great majority of our churches, to use it would be at present wrong. Are churches in this position to be cut off from the Catholic practice of the celebration of the Holy Eucharist with the normal com-plement of sacred ministers, just because Rome in recent times departed from the custom of the rest of the Church ? We have sometimes heard a great deal about the importance of following the "general practice of the Church" as a whole ; it is strange that in this particular matter of the three sacred ministers Catholic custom has been so lightly esteemed and so freely disregarded.

In churches where the parson has no assistant curate he has to sing the principal parts of the service by himself ; but even in places of this kind there is (or ought to be) an educated parish clerk in reader's orders, who could read the epistle. Nor is there any ancient rule or custom which prevents the use of incense at a service of this kind if it be considered desirable.

Where there is a second priest, or a deacon, the full complement of the three ministers can be made up by such a clerk as we have mentioned, acting as subdeacon.[1] At the principal service of the day one ought never to see a priest

See Appendix 1, p 69, "The Readers of the Gospel and Epistle"

or deacon merely present in choir while the celebrant is only assisted by servers.

It is needless to say that a solemn celebration of the Holy Eucharist allows considerable scope for ceremonial under favourable circumstances, but it can also take place with very little. The ancient practice of the Church in this part of Europe—in France, indeed, till quite recently, and to some extent in Spain even to-day—allows of great variety in this : there were several grades of High Mass, so to speak.[1] In regard to a great deal, the individual parish priest must be his own guide as to how much he attempts. A full scheme of ceremonial is given in the *Parson's Handbook*, ch. xii ; but the parson need not use all the ceremonies there described—indeed, in many places, it would be disastrous to attempt to do so. We here subjoin the briefest possible outline of how the Holy Eucharist may be celebrated with the three sacred ministers.

OUTLINE OF THE ENGLISH SERVICE

The Preparation and Approach.—The subdeacon, after vesting, should prepare the paten and mix the chalice at the side-altar or at the credence, with the help of the clerk. Both return to the vestry. All then go to the altar, the clerk first (carrying the cross on high days), then the subdeacon, carrying the gospel-book, then the deacon, then the priest.

The three ministers bow towards the altar together when they arrive below the altar-steps, the subdeacon going to the left of the celebrant, the deacon to his right.

Lord's Prayer.—The clergy will now take up their normal position facing east at the north or left part of the front of the altar where the book lies open on its cushion. The normal position of the deacon is immediately behind the priest, that of the subdeacon immediately behind the deacon. But when the priest turns to the people the deacon moves

[1] See *Ceremoniale Parisiense*, 1703, for much detail of this kind, at a comparatively late date. This *Ceremoniale* is that set forth by Cardinal de Noailles, Archbishop of Paris, who corresponded with Dr. Wake, Archbishop of Canterbury, on the possibility of reunion between the French and English Churches.

a little to the right and turns with him, while the subdeacon kneels down ; and during the *Sanctus* and *Gloria* the deacon and subdeacon go up to the altar on either side of the celebrant

Decalogue.—During the Commandments the deacon turns with the priest, and the subdeacon kneels as directed above The Collects may be read from the south side of the altar, in which case the clergy will walk across the steps together and then stand behind one another as before

Epistle.—The clerk hands the epistle-book to the subdeacon, who reads it facing the people, either from the choir-gate or from the south side within the altar-rails (where there used to be a lectern in some churches). The celebrant and the others will sit in the sedilia while it is being read, and continue sitting while the grail, etc., or hymn, is sung. In most churches it is best to sing a sequence or other appropriate hymn

Gospel.—The Gospel may be read from near the choir-gate, or from a lectern on the north side between the choir and the altar. All will, of course, stand, turning towards the deacon while the Gospel is being read.

Creed.—At the Creed all turn to the altar, and the deacon and subdeacon stand right and left of the priest.

Offertory.—After the Sermon, if there be one, the celebrant goes to the Lord's Table and begins the Offertory ; the subdeacon takes the alms bason to the chancel-step for the collection ; meanwhile the clerk goes to the credence or the side altar, and brings first the burse, and then the chalice and paten containing the elements, one on the top of the other, to the celebrant, who (of course *after* the alms have been presented) will place them on the altar, where the deacon will have previously spread the corporal.

After the celebrant has washed his hands, assisted by the subdeacon, he turns to the people and says, *Let us pray for the whole state of Christ's Church,* etc , the deacon turning as well and the subdeacon kneeling. He then turns to the altar, and so do the deacon and subdeacon, all standing in a line, one behind the other.

Confession.—At *Ye that do truly,* the priest turns, and the deacon with him, the subdeacon kneeling : at the confession all kneel, the deacon slightly to the right, so as to make room for the celebrant.

Sursum Corda.—When the priest turns to the people and sings, *Lift up your hearts,* the deacon stands and turns with him, and the subdeacon may also stand and turn, moving slightly to the left. At *It is very meet,* all turn to the altar, standing one behind the other in the middle: at the beginning of the *Sanctus* the deacon goes up to the altar on the priest's right, the subdeacon on the priest's left. At *We do not presume,* all kneel.

Consecration.—During the Consecration the deacon stands beside the priest on his right, and the subdeacon stands at his place behind.[1]

Communion.—The celebrant should himself communicate the subdeacon in both kinds (if the latter receives at this service), before he gives the chalice to the deacon who is to help him in communicating the rest of the clergy and the lay folk.

Post-Communion.—After the Communion the deacon and subdeacon stand in a line behind the celebrant during the Lord's Prayer and the prayer which follows, and they revert to this position if a Post-Communion Collect is said after the *Gloria.* During the *Gloria* they stand at the altar, one on either side of the celebrant. When the priest turns round to say *The peace of God,* they kneel, the deacon somewhat to the right.

Ablutions.—After the Blessing, and when the celebrant has consumed what remains of the Holy Sacrament, the subdeacon gives him the wine and water for the ablutions, which are handed to him by the clerk. Meanwhile the deacon moves the book and its cushion to the north part of the altar. While the celebrant washes his hands the deacon folds up the corporals and puts them in the burse ; the clerk comes forward with the offertory veil and receives from the deacon the chalice and burse, which he carries to the credence or vestry.

The three ministers then descend from the altar, turn

[1] See p. 60, n. 1.

F

round, and bow towards it, and proceed to the vestry in
the order in which they came.

PRIEST AND CLERK ONLY.— Where there is neither
deacon nor subdeacon, the priest will do the deacon's work
and the clerk the subdeacon's as far as possible. But in
most cases it will be found more convenient for the priest to
prepare the chalice and paten, the clerk helping him. The
clerk will read the Epistle, if possible. He will accompany
the priest when he reads the Gospel. He will bring in the
burse and the elements, serve the priest with water to wash
his hands, and give him the ablutions at the end of the
service.[1]

POSITION OF THE CLERK.—At Sarum, and probably in
most cathedral churches, the clerk normally stood in the
middle, behind the subdeacon, and he seems to have followed the gestures of the subdeacon. In smaller churches
it will be found more convenient for him to stand and kneel
on the south side, near the credence. When there are no
deacon and subdeacon, the best place for the clerk would
be before the altar on the deacon's step, rather to the south
side. But these are among the things which have no fixed
rule, and are best arranged by the clergy for their own
particular church.

CONCLUSION. —It is, as we have already indicated,
a mistake to suppose that every solemn celebration must
have an equally full ceremonial. In England of old—indeed
all over the West until quite modern times—the amount of
ceremonial was determined by circumstances. In great
churches more detail was laid down, and the ceremonial,
being greater in quantity, assumed a more definitely local
character. So that in Salisbury Cathedral there was the
fully developed Sarum use, which was, no doubt, taken as
a model *in kind* though not *in quantity,* so to speak. In
London the elaborate ceremonial of the cathedral followed
the local usages of St. Paul's ; at York, those of York ; at

[1] See Appendix I, p. 69, "The Readers of the Gospel and Epistle."

Aberdeen, those of Aberdeen ; at Elgin the full ceremonial
of the Cathedral was supposed to be like that of Salisbury,
but a high mass in a Dorset parish church was very like
a high mass in a London parish church—both followed
general English use, and the more detailed customs of
cathedrals were only copied by the larger churches. There
was a sort of greatest common measure of ceremonial which
was common to the whole of England, and this is what was
followed in the average parish church.

THE CEREMONIAL OF THE SCOTTISH AND AMERICAN LITURGIES

The Scottish Liturgy has been well said to be the best in
the English language. In it the Prayer Book principles of
appeal to primitive or catholic practice are thoroughly
carried out, particularly as regards the order of parts in the
Prayer of Consecration. In the dark days of the eighteenth
century, when the Scottish Church was groaning under
persecution from the Government in England, and was
reduced to "the shadow of a shade," the great learning of
the nonjurors bore splendid fruit in the edition of the
Scottish Liturgy of 1764, which has ever since been used
with only small verbal variations. The Scottish Episcopal
Church of that day, small though it was in numbers, was
untainted with the Protestant neglect so conspicuous in
England at the time. The holy Liturgy was celebrated
with as much care as was possible under circumstances
which admitted of no permanent altar, still less of anything
like a chancel. Although there was no "ceremonial" in
the sense in which the word is now commonly understood,
the older clergy kept up a sound and careful tradition with
regard to many things. This tradition grew up with the
Liturgy and formed part of it, and in the Scottish and
American Churches we ought to follow it as far as it will
take us. It does not provide us with everything we want

now, because our circumstances are no longer those of persecution ; so that for many things, such as the arrangement of the chancel and the altar, and the vestments of the clergy, we must turn to an earlier date, to a time when these things were at their best in Scotland. Unfortunately Scotland suffered a great deal in such matters from bad English influence in the nineteenth century. First there was the inrush of the " qualified," especially in the south of Scotland—Anglican congregations, " qualified " under the civil law, Protestant in doctrine, slovenly in practice, at one time in a schismatical position, though they returned to communion with the lawful bishops Then came the Oxford Movement, which, while it undid much of the mischief caused by the " qualified," and was of the greatest possible value to the Scottish Church, caused men to look to England for ceremonial. This became a source of evil after a time, for there had arisen in England a second generation who, with little real liturgical knowledge, imagined that they had a great deal, and under the pleas of " correctness " and " universal Western use," succeeded in introducing a number of modern Roman liturgical practices of an undesirable kind among unsuspecting Scottish Church people.

In the following simple directions we propose to go behind all this, and to follow nothing but the older Scottish traditions,[1] which have a far stronger claim on Scottish and American Church-people than anything else, and that on purely Catholic grounds.

OUTLINE OF THE SCOTTISH AND AMERICAN SERVICES

Preparation, etc.—The altar should be prepared in accordance with the rules given on pp. 73-75. Although primarily intended for use in England, these rules are in accordance with Scottish tradition The differences between Scottish and English use are of little importance,

---

[1] These have been collected in great detail by Mr F. C. Eeles, for the Alcuin Club Collection, No xvii, *Traditional Ceremonial and Customs connected with the Scottish Liturgy*, 1910

except that in every Scottish church a "Sacrament House" or aumbry for the reserved Sacrament should be provided in the north wall of the sanctuary, or else in the north part of the east wall, between the altar and the north wall—an example which might well be followed all over the Anglican Communion.

The priest should put on his vestments and proceed to the chancel: he bows towards the altar and goes to the credence, where (after washing his hands) he places the bread upon the paten and pours first the wine and then the water into the chalice. (The traditional way of preparing the bread in Scotland was to cut it in square slices, not too thin; these were cut across and across at right angles, but not so deeply as entirely to sever the cubes thus formed. On the top was laid another slice, cut in the form of a cross and similarly divided, which the priest broke when he made the ceremonial fraction. The feeling was intensely strong that the fact of all being partakers of the one bread should be thus emphasized in the ceremonial.) He sets the paten on the top of the chalice, or else on the credence on the left of the chalice, covers both with the upper corporal, and goes to the altar, where he begins the service standing at the north part of the west side.

If, however, he is not going to prepare the paten and chalice until the Offertory, he will, of course, go straight to the altar. There are two traditions regarding this connected with the Scottish Liturgy. The preparation before the service, however, is older—and also better liturgically, being more in accordance with the genius of the rite.

Decalogue and Collects.—He will turn to the people for the Commandments or the Summary of the Law. He may then cross to the south for the Collects.

Epistle and Gospel.—He reads the Epistle from the south side (of course, facing the people) and the Gospel from the north side. For the ascription before the Gospel all turn to the altar.

Creed.—The Creed should be begun and finished in the middle of the altar, the celebrant being careful to bow at

the holy Name   In mediæval Scotland they bowed at *was
incarnate, was made man,* and *was crucified,* and also at *life
of the world to come.*

Offertory [1]—The priest turns to the people for "*Let us
present our offerings,*" etc., if there be no deacon present :
otherwise the deacon says these words.

The elements, of course, must not be placed on the altar
until the alms have been presented [2], for this is contrary to
the rubric in the Liturgy. If they have been prepared
beforehand, they will now be brought. Then the priest,
standing before the middle of the altar, offers them simultaneously with a slight elevation during the form *Blessed
be thou,* finally placing the paten in front and the chalice
behind

Anaphora [3]—He will now turn round towards the people
and say, *The Lord be with you,* turning back to the altar
before saying, "*It is very meet, right,*" etc

He bows slightly at *Holy, Holy, Holy,* and proceeds with
the Consecration without any pause [4], saying the whole of it
in a clear and distinct voice, not too slowly and without any
noticeable pause until after the Invocation, and without any
lowering of the voice at the words of institution. At the
words *He took bread,* he takes the paten into his hands,
breaking the bread at the words *He brake it* : while he says
This is my Body he crosses his hands palm downwards with
the fingers joined, the left hand being uppermost, and so lays
them upon the bread. He elevates the paten very slightly
at the words *Do this*   At the words *He took the cup* he takes
the chalice into his hands, and while he says *This is my
Blood* he lays his hands upon the chalice or chalices joined
in the manner just described, making a slight elevation at
the words *Do this.*

[1] In the Scottish Liturgy   The Offertory in the American Liturgy is the
same as in the English
[2] In the case of the older form of the Scottish rite the alms are offered
during the form *Blessed be thou*   The priest should hold the alms-dish slightly
raised while saying *Blessed be thou,* raising it a little more at the words *Of thine
own do we give unto thee,* and leaving it on the south part of the altar
[3] In the American Liturgy the Canon is after the Confession, etc , as in
the English
[4] In the American Liturgy he kneels first for the Prayer of Access

He continues, *Wherefore, O Lord,* etc., without any pause
or gesture of reverence, and it would be in accordance with
mediæval custom in this part of Europe if he stretched out
his arms *in modum crucis.* At the words *Which we now offer
unto Thee,* he may follow the old nonjuring tradition and
make a considerable elevation of both chalice and paten
simultaneously, the paten in the right hand, the chalice in
the left hand, not, however, raising them above his head.
This is what is done in Russia at the corresponding place
in the liturgies of S. Basil and S. John Chrysostom.[1] In
the modern Scottish rite during the Invocation he should
make the signs of the Cross here indicated : *send thy Holy
Spirit upon us and upon these thy gifts and creatures of bread
and wine, that, being bles✠sed and hallow✠ed by his life-giving
power, they may become the bo✠dy and blo✠od of thy most
dearly beloved Son. . . .* In the American rite the crossings
should be thus : *Vouchsafe to ble✠ss and sanc✠tify, with thy
Wo✠rd and Holy Spir✠it, these thy gifts and creatures of bread
and wine ; that we . . . may be partakers of his most blessed
Bo✠dy and Blo✠od.*

The Consecration is now complete, and the priest should
here make a reverent inclination.

At *Let us pray for the whole state of Christ's Church*[2] the
priest should turn half round by the right ; indeed, whenever the priest turns to the people he should always
remember to turn with the sun. If there be a Deacon he
says these words. He should not turn at all at the words
As our Saviour Christ, etc., before the Lord's Prayer in the
Scottish Liturgy. The people must join in the Lord's
Prayer.

If there be a Deacon he says *Ye that do truly,* but the
priest leads the confession. During the Absolution the
priest raises his right hand extended at the words *Have
mercy,* keeping it so raised to the end, and making the sign
of the Cross at the words *Pardon an✠d deliver.*

[1] In the churches which still use the Scottish rite of 1764 he should make
the signs of the Cross here indicated : *Vouchsafe to ble✠ss and sanc✠tify, with
thy wo✠rd and Holy Spi✠rit, these thy gifts and creatures of bread and wine,
that they may become the Bo✠dy and Blo✠od of thy dearly beloved Son.*

[2] Said before the Canon in the American Liturgy.

In communicating the people he begins at the south end of the rail : each communicant says *Amen*[1] to the words of administration. All the older Church-people in Scotland received with the open right hand resting on the left, and in some places the women cover the *left* hand with a clean handkerchief.

Post-Communion.—At the bidding *Having now received,*[1] after the Communion, which the Deacon says, if one be present, the priest turns to the people : he also turns to them for the whole of the blessing, and makes the sign of the Cross over them at the mention of the Holy Trinity.

After the blessing the priest takes the ablutions in the usual way, making any necessary arrangements for reserving the Sacrament.

[1] This only occurs in the Scottish Liturgy

TWELVE
DRAWINGS OF THE COMMUNION SERVICE
ACCORDING TO THE
ENGLISH, SCOTTISH, AND AMERICAN RITES

G

I

THE END OF THE PROCESSION

BEFORE THE LITURGY

On Sunday morning, Mattins having been said or sung in choir, the Litany is said or sung, and after this is the appointed time for the Holy Communion.[1] In many churches the Litany is sung in procession on ordinary Sundays; and on festivals it is a general custom to sing a hymn for the procession (the Litany having been previously said kneeling, since the rubric and canon do not allow of its omission). In the church here portrayed, incense and portable lights are used for these festival processions, though not for the Litany: it is worth stating again, however, that the Committee of the Alcuin Club fully realizes that incense, lawful as it is, can with wisdom be used only in a small number of churches at the present day.[2]

To avoid overcrowding the picture, the choir, which stands in the chancel for the concluding prayers of the procession, is represented only by two boys and four men. If there were chanters, these would be standing in front of the boys. The priest stands on the pavement before the altar, on his right the deacon or gospeller, on his left the subdeacon or epistoler. They are wearing over their other garments (as throughout the series) the chasuble (which is the *phelones* or *pænula* of the Apostolic age[3]), the dalmatic, and the tunicle respectively. Behind these stands the parish clerk or acolyte, wearing a plain tunicle over his amice and albe, and holding the cross. On either side of him the taperers stand, in amice and albe, holding their tapers.

In churches where a less elaborate service is necessary, the clerk and servers could lawfully wear rochets or surplices.

There are a cross and two lights on the holy Table. Two standards are on the pavement, beyond the ends of the choir-stalls.

[1] See Appendix III, Note 1, " Mattins, Litany, and Holy Communion."
[2] Cf. pp. 29, 30.   [3] See p. 22, n. 2, and p. 48, n. 1.

1. THE END OF THE PROCESSION

II

PREPARATION OF THE ELEMENTS

IN A CHAPEL BEFORE THE SERVICE

In accordance with the Lincoln Judgement the chalice is mixed before the service. The bread naturally is prepared at the same time. This is here done, for motives of convenience, reverence, and publicity in a chapel, where the prepared paten and chalice are left (on the altar) until they are brought up at the Offertory, as shown in Plate VIII.

The subdeacon stands, holding the chalice, into which the clerk is pouring wine and water from the cruets. (It may be better, in places where there is sufficient light, for the chalice to remain on the altar, the subdeacon holding it steady while the wine and water are poured in.) The taperers are supposed to be out of sight on the right, near the credence of the chapel (also not seen in the picture) on which would be standing a canister of bread, and the bowl, ewer, and towel which the subdeacon has used for washing his hands. Both subdeacon and clerk wear apparelled amices and albes, the subdeacon being distinguished by his tunicle. In places where greater simplicity is required, the clerk would wear a surplice or rochet.[1]

The chapel altar is vested in the usual way, the frontal, frontlet, fair linen, and the cross and candlesticks being visible. Behind it is a plain dorsal, flanked by two riddels, which hang from rods bearing sconces with candles at the ends. This altar stands against the east wall of the south aisle. On the left, part of the chancel-screen can be seen, with a figure in surplice and hood, who stands in a returned stall, joining in a hymn or introit. Beyond him the high altar can be seen: in our ancient Gothic churches there would be a window immediately above the dorsal of this altar; but many modern churches have a bare wall-space.

[1] See Appendix II, "Plan," p. 77.

44

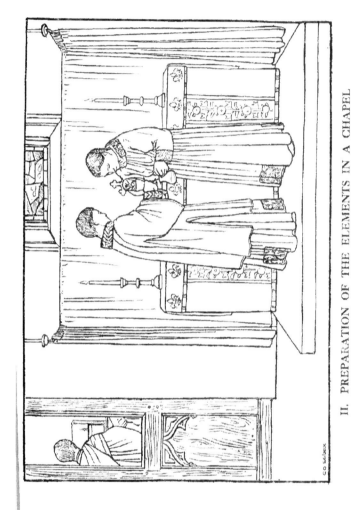

II. PREPARATION OF THE ELEMENTS IN A CHAPEL

III

THE DECALOGUE

The priest, at the north end of the Lord's Table reads the Ten Commandments. The deacon stands on his own step, facing the same way, since he always turns with the priest. The subdeacon, kneels on his lower step, facing east. The clerk stands in his usual place near the southern part of the altar, facing across. The taperers stand on the pavement, north and south.

As all the vestments are shown in this picture, it may be convenient to enumerate them here once for all:— *Priest*, amice, albe, girdle, crossed stole, fanon or maniple, chasuble or phelonion ; *Deacon*, amice, albe, girdle, stole worn over left shoulder, maniple, dalmatic ; *Subdeacon*, amice, albe, girdle, maniple, tunicle ; *Clerk*, amice, albe, girdle, tunicle ; *Taperers*, amice, albe, girdle. All the amices and albes are represented as apparelled, which is beautiful but not a necessity in the case of the albe. A Ψ shaped orphrey is suggested on the chasuble, and orphreys of the ancient *clavus* type on the dalmatic and tunicle, with an apparel on the dalmatic.

A window of the old kind, coming down to the dorsal, is shown in this picture: in Perpendicular architecture the window would be somewhat wider. The dorsal and riddels are of the same type as in Plate II, with riddel-rods and sconces. The frontal and frontlet are extremely plain, but with good bold fringes. Cushions are seen on the holy Table, and two lights. The taperers' candlesticks stand before them: they are made to drop into weighted bases, and have each a decorated grip.

The proper levels are clearly shown—foot-pace, deacon's step, subdeacon's step, and pavement: they are of the best proportions, broad and low. It will be observed that the carpet in front of the Communion table is in these pictures either suggested in outline or omitted altogether, in order to avoid confusion.

III. THE DECALOGUE

47

IV

THE COLLECTS

The parish clerk and taperers have not changed their places; but the three chief ministers have gone to the south end of the altar, and the priest stands, with hands uplifted (his attitude being an unbroken tradition from the second century—doubtless from the apostolic age itself —as is shown by the numberless figures of *orantes* in the Catacombs of Rome),[1] to say the Collect for Church and King and the Collect of the day. The gospeller and epistoler are behind him, each on his own step: this is the normal arrangement of the three ministers in times of prayer.

The frontal and frontlet are more ornate than in the last picture, and so also are the orphreys of the vestments. Lights, cross, and cushions are shown on the altar. The dorsal and riddels are carried on three rods, which are suspended on four riddel-posts—this beautiful arrangement being here clearly shown. The posts are finished into capitals in which sconces for candles are fixed.

In this illustration all the lights (except that of the first taperer) are seen. They may therefore be enumerated here:—Two upon the altar (not upon a gradine, which is a still common error);[2] four upon the four riddel-posts; two on standards which stand upon the pavement (not upon a step); the two lights of the taperers, which are set down in front of them. There could lawfully be fewer lights (e.g., only the two on the altar), or more (e.g., additional standards in a large church, tapers on brackets in the wall, or additional lights on the riddel-posts, rails, or entablature, or on candelabra hanging from the roof), but never more than two on the altar.

[1] The reader will hardly need reminding that in these ancient pictures, the *orantes* both male and female, generally wear either the pænula (now called the chasuble), the dalmatic, or the tunic, these garments being every-day articles of attire in the first and succeeding centuries. (See pp. 22, 54.) Examples will be found in *The Ornaments of the Ministers*, Mowbray, 1908.

[2] See Appendix, "Plan of Sanctuary," pp. 73-4.

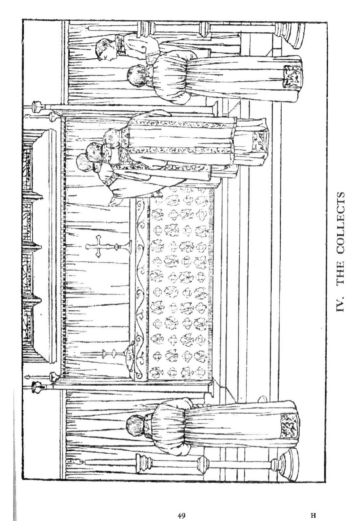

IV. THE COLLECTS

V

THE EPISTLE

The subdeacon stands at the top of the chancel-step, facing the people, to read the Epistle. The priest sits in the easternmost sedile (his proper place), next him the deacon: the vacant sedile of the subdeacon is hidden by the standing figure of the clerk, who will generally find it convenient to sit or stand nearer the deacon than is here shown (especially if books are handed out for a sequence or other hymn, etc.), if indeed he does not sit in the subdeacon's seat

It will be noticed that the designs of the ornaments are different. The epistoler's tunicle is without orphreys. The plain frontlet of the altar contrasts well with the bold design of the frontal. There is a figure upon the cross. A piscina is shown in the south wall.

In this and the next plate, a shallow chancel, such as exists in many churches, is shown in order that the artist may keep his figures together. The choir may be supposed to occupy a west gallery. West galleries it may be mentioned, are not all of the Georgian period: there are beautiful mediaeval examples, for instance, in Norfolk.

V. THE EPISTLE

51

VI

THE GOSPEL

The deacon stands at the lectern facing the people. The subdeacon stands behind the lectern, to hold the leaf down or turn it over if necessary. The clerk stands behind the subdeacon, holding a cross on festivals. The taperers hold their lights on either side of the lectern. The thurifer (dressed like the taperers) swings the censer in a convenient place (behind the subdeacon, when there is room enough). All stand so as not to hide the gospeller's face from the people

The only other points requiring comment are the conveniently-shaped Communion benches (which are represented without the white linen houseling-cloths thrown over them), and another extremely useful piece of furniture, the folding lectern, on the top of which lies a strip of richly-decorated material. A Sacrament-house might have been sketched on the north wall, or there might be one or two aumbries on this or on the east wall.

It may be remarked that, if the design of the frontal looks almost "over-bold" in the picture, this is due to its being in black-and-white In colours the pattern would not be too conspicuous; indeed the fault of most frontals is that the design is hardly seen.

As was pointed out under Plate V, the artist has drawn an exceptionally shallow chancel, in order to avoid having to show the altar or sedilia at a distance and on a small scale. These two pictures might be taken to represent the chapel of some school or community.

VI. THE GOSPEL

53

VII
THE END OF THE CREED
BEFORE THE SERMON

The three ministers are standing at the Creed before the holy Table in their normal positions for acts of praise and worship, i.e. the priest at the midst of the altar, the deacon on his right and the subdeacon on his left, all three being on the footpace. The clerk can also be seen, facing the altar,[1] and one of the taperers.

The preacher, wearing surplice, hood, and tippet over his cassock,[2] is being conducted from his stall by the verger, who wears a gown over his cassock, and carries the rod of his office. The preacher will be in the pulpit before the end of the Creed, and will there give out notices, say the Bidding, and preach, the three ministers sitting meanwhile in the sedilia.[3] If Warning is to be read of Communion, one of the ministers may come to the chancel-step, for this purpose, at the conclusion of the sermon.[4]

In a church with only two clergy present the deacon (or priest) would himself be the preacher, having left the altar and taken off his dalmatic (or chasuble) and maniple, and the clerk would be standing where the subdeacon is. If there are three clergy present, the preacher of course may be either deacon or subdeacon or priest; and where the priest is single-handed he had best take off his chasuble, inconspicuously, near the sedilia.

Should a church of old-fashioned traditions desire to restore the Eucharist as the great act of evangelical worship, but with as little change as possible, the servers would be dispensed with ; and the clerk would attend upon the priest, wearing a surplice. The priest would wear a plain albe, and over it a large and plain chasuble, or *phelones*, recalling thus to his congregation, as we have already suggested, the cloke which St. Paul left at Troas.[5] Or he could wear a cope, though this might strike his congregation as ritualistic. Deacon and subdeacon might be in surplices. The preacher might wear his walking-dress, viz. a gown and tippet over his cassock ; but he would hardly find it convenient to do this if he is taking part in the service itself.

A plain rood-screen is suggested in the picture, hiding the ends of the altar from the spectator. There is a pleasant arrangement of panelling on the east wall, and a piscina on the south. There might be also a Sacrament-house or aumbry on the north wall.

[1] The common phrase "turning to the East for the Creed" is rather misleading. People turn "to the altar" for this and other acts of faith and praise : therefore the clerk does not confront the east wall in this picture.

[2] The hood in the picture is of the true shape, made with a cape, this cape being however rather small, and of what may be called perhaps a transitional type, to avoid the appearance of strangeness. The tippet is also of the shape which it had before it was spoilt by the tailors, viz., a long strip of the full breadth of the silk, not doubled, nor crushed in any way, but worn loosely in its natural folds.

[3] See Appendix III, Note 2, "The Sermon."

[4] See Appendix III, Note 3, "Warning of Communion."

[5] See Introductory Picture and p. 48.

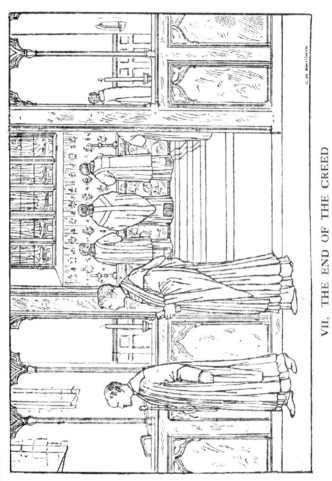

VII. THE END OF THE CREED

VIII

THE OFFERTORY

BRINGING IN THE ELEMENTS, OR "THE GREAT ENTRANCE"

The alms have been collected, received by the subdeacon or deacon, presented by the priest, and laid upon the altar[1]: the clerk now brings solemnly from the chapel, where they were prepared before the service, the paten and chalice containing the bread and wine for the Eucharist. This impressive and significant procession we have ventured to call by the name of "The Great Entrance," by which it is called in the Orthodox Church of the East, where the ancient custom of preparing the elements in a special chapel has never been lost.

The deacon and subdeacon stand at their usual places, south and north of the priest, awaiting the arrival of the eucharistic elements. These are carried in the chalice and paten by the clerk, whose hands are muffled in the large offertory veil (there being no other chalice veil). The clerk's tunicle in this picture is ornamented by a single "pillar" orphrey. He is preceded by the taperers, and in this case by a second clerk (also in a tunicle) carrying a cross. A second clerk may assist in cathedral and other large churches on festal Sundays: he may stand, when not employed, near the north of the altar, facing across. In other churches, and on ordinary Sundays, the cross may be dispensed with; though a thurifer or other minister might carry the cross, if there were no second clerk and the use of a cross were desired.

The ornaments are similar to those in former plates, and call for no special notice.

[1] The alms-bason is hidden by the deacon in the picture.

VIII. THE OFFERTORY

IX

THE GENERAL CONFESSION

All kneel, in accordance with the rubric, to join with humble voice in the Confession, which in the English rite is led by the deacon, but in the Scottish and American rites by the priest himself. They occupy their usual places, each of the ministers kneeling on his own steps. The orphreys and apparels in this picture are of elaborate design

The figures, taking them from left to right, are—Second taperer, subdeacon, priest, deacon, first taperer, clerk.

For the simple form of village service, eliminate all the figures, except the priest, and dress the clerk in a surplice, as his sole assistant, at the place here occupied by the deacon. To enhance the simplicity, imagine the priest vested without albe-apparels in a plain chasuble, such as is shown in the Introductory Picture, and, of reduced form, in Plate XI.

The altar in this picture has the riddels carried on rods (but always, as is right, parallel to the ends of the holy Table, and not spread out), and there are no posts in this example. The frontal has six panels, and the frontlet a graceful running design.

The artist has represented cushions on the altar: but a single desk would be equally right, though rather less decorative.

IX. THE GENERAL CONFESSION

59

X

THE PRAYER OF CONSECRATION

The priest stands at the midst of the altar to consecrate the holy Mysteries. The deacon and subdeacon are on his right and left, their usual places, each on his own step.[1] The clerk stands reverently at his usual place : (a second clerk would be exactly opposite to him, facing south [2]). The taperers stand in the midst of the chancel, between the choir-stalls ; but here a shallow chancel is suggested, so as to avoid diminishing the scale of the altar.[3]

The chalice and paten, with the altar-lights, are hidden by the ministers.

The other ornaments call for no comment, beyond that given under former plates ; but the reader may be reminded that in many beautiful examples (especially in the case of altars by Mr. Comper) angels are set on the four riddel-posts, each angel sometimes holding a taper ; and also that a carved and gilt cornice may stretch from post to post, round the three sides of the altar, as in the fine altar by the St. Dunstan Society, at Lancing College Chapel. An admirable example of the use of angels on the riddel-posts, the high altar at St. John's, Newcastle-on-Tyne, designed by Sir Charles Nicholson, is given at the beginning of this book.[4]

[1] Fortunately perhaps, there is no very constant tradition as to the assistants' place at this point. In the Scottish and American rites, the deacon would assist the priest and stand immediately on his right. In our service, if the priest prefers to be alone at this solemn time, the deacon may legitimately stand behind him, while the subdeacon may always take the central position on his own step.

[2] See under Plate VIII.

[3] Cf. under Plates V and VI.

[4] See frontispiece.

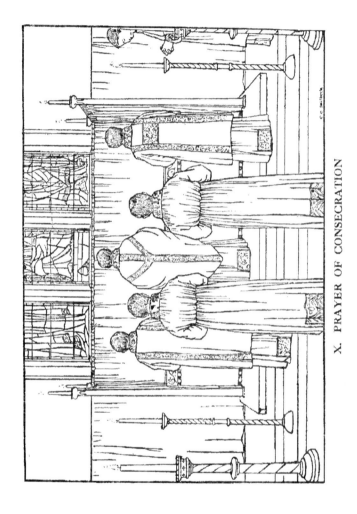

X. PRAYER OF CONSECRATION

61

XI

"GLORIA IN EXCELSIS"

The Communion of the people being over,[1] all stand, each in the place and posture normal for an act of praise. The priest is raising his hands to begin the *Gloria in Excelsis*; they are joined after the opening sentence. The taperers have come back during the priest's communion to the pavement of the sanctuary (this movement having been a sign for the communicants to approach); during the communion of the people they faced across, standing further apart than usual: they now are back in their normal positions

In this picture the priest wears a plain chasuble, and the other vestments are also without orphreys. The most beautiful type of chasuble is doubtless that which approximates most to the original pænula and to the earlier mediæval type—plain, and larger than that here shown.

It may be noted here that orphreys have no special significance, and may be varied a good deal. A chasuble may have a rich border and no other ornament (the most usual form in mediæval brasses), or a Y or Ψ orphrey, or a Latin cross or straight pillar as a matter of custom, however, the Latin cross is to be deprecated, because it bears no relation to the folds of the chasuble and leads to the degradation of its shape. The dalmatic may have two or four apparels, or none; the same may be said of the tunicle; and either may have single or double orphreys, or not, and laced cords and tassels, or not.

The altar in this example has two riddel-posts only; the rod of the dorsal being fixed by hooks (unseen) to the wall.

[1] See Appendix, Note 4, "The Communion and the Communicants"

XI. GLORIA IN EXCELSIS

63

XII

THE BLESSING

After the Communion, the sacred Elements have been covered, in accordance with the rubric, with a fair linen cloth, this being the folded pall, now spread over the Elements as a second corporal. The Post-Communion prayer has been said, and the priest turns and raises his hand to give the Blessing. The others all kneel, at their usual places.

Thus the holy service is concluded; and, after the clerk has carried the vessels out, the other ministers return to the vestry in the order in which they came.

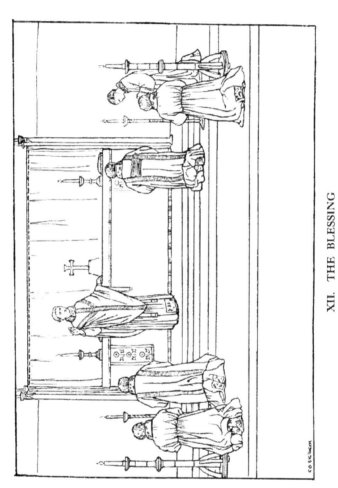

XII. THE BLESSING

K

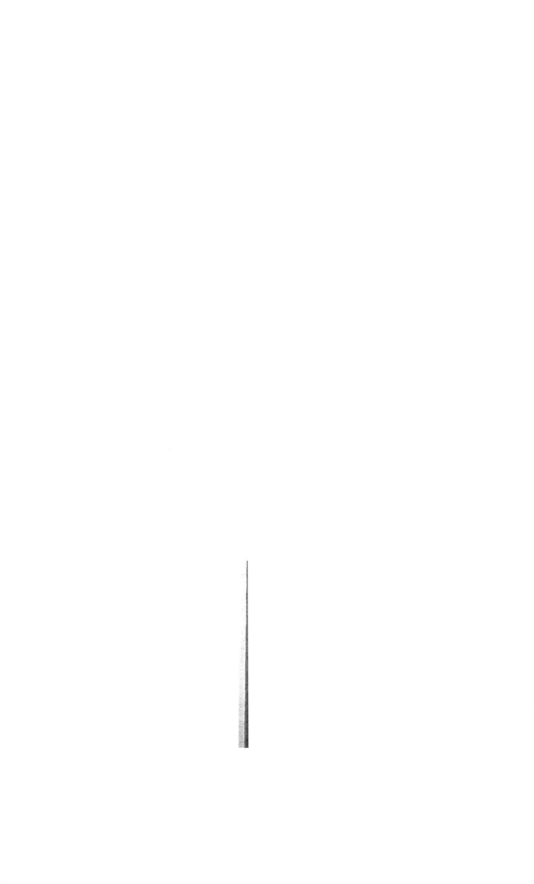

APPENDICES

APPENDIX I

THE READERS OF THE GOSPEL AND EPISTLE

In the primitive Church, ministers below the diaconate read both Epistle and Gospel, much as they now read both lessons at Mattins and Evensong In course of time, because of the honour given to the liturgical Gospel, its reading became restricted to deacons.   This restriction has been accepted both in East and West for many centuries, excepting only in the very rare case of certain kings taking the deacon's place.   But no such restriction has ever been accepted as regards the Epistle. Throughout the East the Epistle is ordinarily read by the Reader—to all intents and purposes a layman—not even by the subdeacon.   And all over the West a clerk can take the subdeacon's place, and still does so when necessary. The English parish clerk of old was expected to read the Epistle, and, when needful, to act as subdeacon. There is ample evidence of this—e g., at Elmsted, 1411 ; Coventry, 1462 , Faversham, 1506   Sometimes the Epistle seems to have been read by an ordinary layman.

There was no alteration of this at the Reformation.   In the First Prayer Book the rubric says, "the priest, or he that is appointed, shall read the Epistle"; "the priest or deacon then shall read the Gospel."   A companion book to the 1549 Prayer Book was issued for the use of the clerk, and in it the reading of the Epistle is explicitly stated to be one of the things that pertains to his office.   Nor was any change made afterwards, for although the rubric since 1552 was abridged to "the priest shall read the Epistle," it goes on to say that he, too, shall read the Gospel.   This is evidently a mere abridgement ; if interpreted otherwise, it would exclude a deacon or even another priest from reading either Epistle or Gospel, which would be absurd in itself, and impossible in face of the Canons of 1604, which provide for gospeller and epistoler, and our present Ordinal which assumes their continuance. Moreover, the old custom went on. In 1571 at York, and in 1576 at Canterbury, Archbishop Grindal required in Visitation Articles that the clerk " be able to read the first lesson, the Epistle, and the Psalms, with answers to the suffrages, *as is used.*" The italics are ours, and the clause should be noted, for it evidently refers to what was common usage. Other post-Reformation Visitation Articles contain much the same. In the seventeenth century the clerks in certain Cathedrals seem to have gone outside their province, and to have read the Gospel. Archbishop Laud, wishing to stop this abuse, went beyond his powers, and in a somewhat high-handed manner forbade them to read the Epistle also. But this was only the action of one man, and cannot for a moment be compared with the evidence on the other side   The zeal of the Laudian school undoubtedly out-ran discretion at times, as witness the manner of the introduction of the 1637 Prayer Book into Scotland. When the clerk in England fell on evil days and became unlearned, he naturally could not take his proper part ; but there were exceptions, and the Epistle continued to be read by the clerk in a few places in England until within living memory. The custom is now being revived in many churches, for a very determined effort is being made to secure that it shall not be allowed to die out. Much of what the clerk did of old, and what the reader does in the East, is now done by our " lay readers " of to-day, who go further, and read the second lesson at Mattins and Evensong, even when taken from the Gospels ; and they ought assuredly not to be forbidden to read the Epistle. Whether it would be wise to allow this explicitly by rubric, or even to encourage it in all circumstances, is another matter. We must not be understood as urging this ; but we do urge, and most emphatically, that it would be a retrograde step to attempt to exclude by rubric that which no part of the Church has ever forbidden. The fact that this custom was not practised by the Nonjurors, and that mid-Victorian churchmen were unfamiliar with it, does not show that it is wrong. It only shows that these good people were inclined to be ultra-sacerdotal in their ideas of the nature of the lessons in the first part of the Communion service. We see the same tendency in the way in which some have encouraged the people to kneel during the Epistle and have read both Epistle and Gospel towards the East, as if they were leading the people in prayer, instead of reading lessons to them.

APPENDIX II

PLAN

SHOWING A CONVENIENT ARRANGEMENT OF THE EAST END OF A TOWN CHURCH

Drawn by Vivian H. King, A.R.I.B.A.

This plan has been drawn in order to help architects and others in the designing of new churches, where the conveniences obtainable at the present day can be provided. The Sanctuary, Choir, and Chapel in the plan will also serve to illustrate the arrangements possible in an old church ; and many of the details can be adapted to existing buildings.

The numbers give the different levels, rising at " 1 " from the floor of the nave and chapel.

The explanation which follows deals only with the Sanctuary and Chapel, and does not touch such matters as vestries, cupboards, etc., which indeed need no further explanation, and are included for their practical value.

EXPLANATION OF THE PLAN

Altar. In later Gothic churches the altars were often longer than the ten feet here given for the high altar : on the other hand, the altars of the English Church during the seventeenth and eighteenth centuries, fine works of art as they often were, ran to the

THE ORNAMENTS OF THE RUBRIC CORRESPONDING TO THE PLAN

The *Altar* or *Holy Table.* Little importance is to be attached to the material or construction of the altar. The wooden table on four legs, draped at least in service time, which is so familiar to us at the present day, was the common form in the early ages of the Church ; though stone

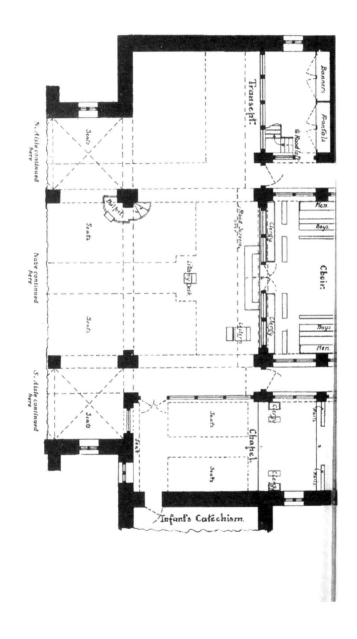

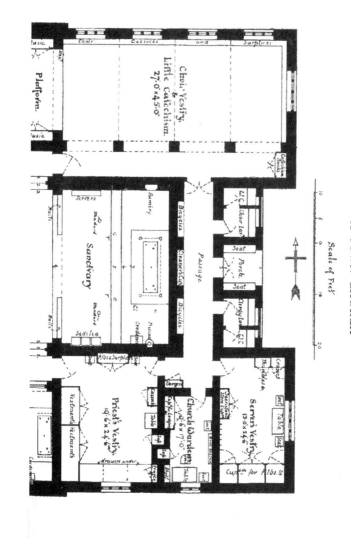

PLAN SHOWING A CONVENIENT ARRANGEMENT OF THE EAST END OF
A TOWN CHURCH

Scale of Feet

opposite extreme of shortness; they were often so short as to resemble the nearly square table of the sixth and seventh century Italian mosaics (e.g. S. Vitale, Ravenna). As a general rule it may be said that a low reredos requires a long altar for proper dignity of proportion, while the ciborium of basilican architecture requires a short altar. The most convenient height for the altar is 3 ft. 3 in.

The high altar in the plan stands at some distance from the east wall, an arrangement which has many practical advantages; the general custom, however, in England during the Gothic period was to place the altar against the east wall, as it is here shown in the chapel. Both methods are given in order to guard against the idea that English Churchmen are restricted to any particular architectural style; and for the same reason the windows and piers are purposely left indeterminate in the plan.

The position of the candles on the holy Table is shown by two small circles in the plan. There is no ground for the common idea that it is illegal for them to stand

gradually came to be preferred because of its durability, and the Council of Epaon ordered the altars to be of stone in Gaul as early as A.D. 573.

A *Frontal* "of silk or other decent stuff." Canon 82 of 1604, in enforcing this among the minimum of ornaments, makes it clear that the disuse "in time of Divine service" of this primitive, and in the second year of Edward VI still universal, ornament is illegal.

A *Frontlet*, or narrow strip of material to cover the suspension of the frontal: it is tacked to one of the linen undercloths.

A "*fair linen cloth* at the time of the Ministration," to which the Ornaments Rubric must add two shorter undercloths of coarse linen covering the altar-slab.

A *Cushion*, or desk, or two cushions for the book.

Two Candles on the altar. This use of two candles is most desirable; yet it cannot be maintained that they are essential ornaments of the rubric. The only requirement of the ancient Canon law was that no Eucharist should be celebrated without a light of some sort; and

L

on the altar itself: on the contrary, this was the custom whenever altar-lights were used both before and after the Reformation, and the only lights declared legal both by the Court of Arches and by Archbishop Benson's Court are the two "standing on the holy Table." It will be noticed that no gradine is shown, the gradine being an unauthorized addition.

The high altar in the plan is surrounded on three sides by curtains (the dorsal and riddels), which are carried on three rods (two short and one long), supported on four slender columns or posts. This is a very beautiful arrangement, but it is not at all essential: the short rods may be fixed on the wall (as in the chapel); or they will be dispensed with altogether if no riddels are used. Or, if there is a reredos' immediately above the altar, no long rod will be wanted, since the reredos will take the place of the upper frontal. It will be noticed in the plan that the riddels in both cases are at right angles to the wall and parallel with the ends of the altar: they ought not to be spread out. In ancient

often this took the form of a single taper standing on the altar or held by the clerk.   Still two lights are certainly best, though there should never be more than two either on the altar or on any shelf or gradine behind it (see also the next paragraph).

A *Dorsal*, or upper frontal with or without two *Riddels*, or a *Reredos* and two riddels; or a reredos only.   The normal height of the reredos or dorsal (the reredos being of stone and the dorsal of silk or stuff) in pre-Reformation churches was not more than about three feet, and sometimes less.   When (as in cathedral churches or college chapels) there was no east window above the altar, a high screen filled with statuary was often built; but even then there was generally some upper frontal or reredos about three feet high to form the usual rich setting for the altar.   When, as in many modern churches, there is a high reredos or wall-space behind the altar, it is generally the best plan to have

¹ See frontispiece.

times the altar was enshrined in a *ciborium*, a canopy resting on four pillars, with architraves or rods between to carry four curtains which completely enshrined the altar at certain parts of the service : in Gothic times the four pillars were sometimes retained, with three of the curtains (the front of the altar being only curtained off in Lent); and sometimes the two short rods with their riddels were the only remnant of the old arrangement; and sometimes even these were dispensed with.

Piscina. A drain through which the water at the lavatory is poured. A shelf is sometimes fixed across the upper part of the arch in which the piscina stands.

Credence. A table on which the elements stand after they are prepared. It will be noticed that ample room is given in the plan for the high altar and its adjuncts. Architects who build small sanctuaries make a quiet, dignified, and reverent ceremonial extremely difficult.

Aumbry. A cupboard often found in old churches, standing about four feet from the ground; and useful either for reserving the Sacrament

a dorsal immediately above the altar, standing well away from this reredos (as in the plan) and flanked with riddels. Candles may be fixed on sconces at one or both ends of the two rods that hold the riddels. When the rods are fixed in the wall, they can of course only carry sconces at the ends farthest from the wall; but when they rest on pillars, four sconces can be carried.

The *bason* and *jug* for the lavatory. These may be of any convenient size or material. The *towel* for the lavatory should be large.

The *chalice* and *paten*. A *wine-cruet* or *flagon*, and a *water-cruet*. A *canister* for the bread. A *burse* containing two *corporals*. An *offertory veil* for the clerk to use in bringing the vessels to the altar at the Offertory.

In Scottish and other dioceses where reservation for the sick is practised, a *pyx* for the reserved Sacrament to stand in the aumbry, or or for keeping plate under lock and key

7 *Footpace*, on which the altar rests.[1] The figure is placed where the priest usually stands.

Cl A convenient place in a parish church for the *Clerk* to stand, when there are deacon and subdeacon.

6. *The Deacon's Step*, his usual position being immediately behind the priest. This step and that of the subdeacon should be broad for convenience in standing

5. The *Subdeacon's Step*, his usual position being behind the deacon. This step and the deacon's are sometimes returned at right angles, for economy in building the levels.

T. T. Position of the *Taperers*, who stand, the right-hand taperer on the left of his candle, and the left-hand taperer on the right of his.

Standards. The position of the two Standards is arranged so that they and the taperers' lights converge towards the lights upon the holy table.

Sedilia for priest, deacon,

to be suspended above the altar

A *carpet* for the footpace; not a hassock. An *amice, albe, girdle, stole, fanon* (or maniple), *and chasuble* for the priest

An *amice, albe, girdle*, and *tunicle* for the clerk (or a *rochet* or *surplice*).

An *amice, albe, girdle, stole fanon*, and *dalmatic* (i.e. tunicle) for the deacon. (Where all the proper vestments are not worn, the priest and deacon would wear surplices and stoles.)

An *amice, albe, girdle, fanon*, and *tunicle*, for the subdeacon. (Where the proper vestments are not worn, the subdeacon would wear a surplice without a stole.)

Amices, albes, and *girdles* (or *rochets* or *surplices*) for the taperers. Two *candles* with *candlesticks* to stand on the ground.

Two large standard *candlesticks* with two *candles* therein. All candles should be of pure wax without either wooden stock or tin shield.

Cushions for the sedilia,

[1] For the dimensions of this and other architectural features in connection with the altar, see the small and most practical book by Harold C King, *The Chancel and the Altar*, London, Mowbrays (Arts of the Church Series), 1911

and subdeacon, that to the east being for the priest [1] It is a good plan to have a fourth sedile for the clerk, as is found in some old churches Movable seats are shown, standing in a recess, which is perhaps the most convenient arrangement.

A *Bench* for the servers is drawn opposite the sedilia.

Communion Rails. Wooden rails broad at the top after the seventeenth-century pattern are here suggested, as being comelier and more convenient than thin rails of brass. Gates are often included, but the sanctuary is better without them, and they are not marked here.

4. *Communicants' Step.* It is important that there should be only one step, so that the communicants can kneel on the level of the pavement.

N. (in the Chapel). *Normal Position* of clerk when there is only one server. In churches where the priest is single-handed this would apply also to the high altar at the principal Eucharist [2]

and *hangings* for the back of the recess. In old churches where the seats are of stone and fixed, hangings and cushions are very necessary Dyed linen is a good material for this purpose, as it does not hold the dust.

Benches or *seats* in any place convenient.

A movable *kneeling-bench* was used before the introduction of *rails*, which seem to have been a Laudian innovation enforced by the Bishops of the period. *Houseling cloths* to cover the rails or bench at the time of Communion.

A *carpet* or *cushion* for the communicants to kneel upon. This is generally now made in the form of a strip of carpet.

By this server a *tunicle*, etc., may be worn (especially if this be the principal or only Eucharist on Sunday); but a simple *rochet* or *surplice* is generally preferable at the present day.

[1] There is no authority for a special episcopal seat in a parish church
[2] No organ is shown on the plan The organ might be placed over the space to the north of the choir, unless the singers occupy a western gallery, which in a modern church would be most conveniently built over a narthex.

APPENDIX III

NOTES

1 MATTINS, LITANY, AND THE COMMUNION

Mattins and Evensong are the services appointed to be said "daily throughout the year": their public recitation in church is the most obvious of the parson's duties, and it is declared to be such over and over again in the Prayer Book. These offices end with the Third Collect, after which is an anthem, with certain prayers, which are either optional or occasional. The priest may use those which are optional, he *must* use those which are occasional at the appointed times. These are: At Mattins on Monday, Tuesday, Thursday, Saturday—Prayer for All Conditions. At Mattins or Evensong (or at both) through Ember Week (i.e. Sunday to Saturday)—Ember Collect. During Session of Parliament (presumably each day)—Prayer for Parliament.

The Prayer for All Conditions is probably intended only for morning use. At Evensong it is a good practice to use instead the General Thanksgiving, the occasions for which are not fixed. The Prayer of S. Chrysostom and the Grace must be said after the occasional prayers, and are therefore conveniently used to conclude Mattins and Evensong on all occasions when the Litany is not appointed to be said.

On Sunday, however, as on Wednesday and Friday, Mattins *must* end at the Third Collect, because the Litany is "appointed to be said." The Ember Prayer and the Prayer for Parliament are on Sunday, Wednesday, and Friday, incorporated in the Litany before the Prayer of S. Chrysostom and the Grace.

The *Litany* must be said on Sunday, Wednesday, and Friday, and after Mattins, which strictly means before the

Holy Communion; for the intention of the Prayer Book
certainly is that Mattins should be said before the Eucharist
at "the beginning of this day" and not late in the morning.
The inference is that Wednesday and Friday (not Tuesday
and Thursday) are the proper days for additional Eucharists
in churches where there is a celebration on three days in
the week, an inference which is borne out by the First
Prayer Book and the older Missals. There is much spiritual
loss when the Litany is misplaced from its position as a
preparation for Communion, and some inconvenience results
from such dislocation of the services.

Any clerk may read the Litany as far as the Lord's Prayer,
when the priest's part begins. No position is assigned for
the reader of this office: the processional use—beautiful
though it be—is probably only convenient for a minority
of churches as yet. In parish churches where it is not
sung in procession, it is best to treat the Litany as a short
and quiet preparatory devotion, saying it without note at
a reading-desk in the nave.

The *Holy Communion* is to be administered on those days
for which Collect, Epistle, and Gospel are provided, *i.e.* on
every Sunday and Holy-day, unless there be a dearth of
communicants. It has taken a long time to recover from the
bad mediæval custom of only communicating once a year;
but nowadays the primitive principle of frequent communion
is happily restored among the devout, and the parishes where
a "convenient number" of people are not ready to communicate every Sunday and Holy-day must be comparatively
few. Such parishes are obviously in need of some years'
steady teaching, and probably of a parochial mission as well.
In every parish the first part of the Communion Service
must be said on all Sundays and Holy-days, and the priest
must go on to consecrate the Eucharist if there be a convenient number "according to his discretion." His only
excuse for not doing this is when communicants have not
signified their names to him at least some time the day
before: the remedy therefore lies in the hand of the laity,
and they should be reminded of this, so that every regular
communicant on going to live in a new parish should at

once write to the priest, announcing his desire to communicate on every Sunday and Holy-day.

The Eucharist is clearly the principal Sunday service;
for it is after the Nicene Creed that the Sermon is to be
preached, the notices of Holy-days and Fasting-days to be
given out, other proclamations to be made, and the Banns
to be published (the last has been illegally erased from the
rubric by the printers). If this be properly done, and yet
the people withdraw from the service when the Sermon
or Church Militant Prayer is over, the priest should read
the Second Exhortation, warning them, "Lest ye, with-
drawing yourselves from this Holy Supper, provoke God's
indignation against you," and exhorting them to stay and
make their Communion. He may also point out that the
rubric describes the Blessing as the permission to depart,
and that Canon 18 forbids them "to depart out of the
Church during the time of Service or Sermon without
some urgent or reasonable cause "

It is therefore unlawful (a) to celebrate Holy Communion
without communicants, three at the very least; (b) to run
this risk through slackness in asking for due notice from
communicants; (c) to have the Sermon, Notices, etc. at
Mattins, with a Celebration at some other time; (d) to
have Mattins, Ante-Communion, and Sermon together,
with the actual Celebration at some other time; (e) to
interrupt the Communion Service after the Sermon or
Church Militant Prayer, by the interpolation of a Blessing,
by the exit of the clergy and choir, or by encouraging the
people to withdraw themselves from this Holy Supper by
the playing of a voluntary and other devices. Either the
service must be continued or it must be closed: it cannot
lawfully be closed and then resumed.

No doubt much teaching will be required before the
above ideal of lawfulness is realized; but the first step is
for every one to be clearly shown that it is the ideal—the
only lawful order for English Churchmen. If the priest
is doing his best with tact and charity, and finds that his
people are difficult to move, he may take comfort from the
thought that the first step is gained when they realize that

they are below the standard of the law, and that for his own part he will be judged not by what his parish is, but by what it is becoming.

It is true that often the lateness of the hour is a difficulty for communicants; but it lies with the clergy to encourage an earlier hour for Mattins, Litany, and Eucharist. All false steps, such as starting a midday Eucharist, should therefore be avoided; and in any readjustment the ideal of 9 a m. should be kept steadily in view.

Holy Communion may be celebrated on any other day of the week, so long as there are communicants, a convenient number at the priest's discretion. A note at the beginning of the Prayer Book provides for this by allowing the Epistle and Gospel (as well as the Collect) of the Sunday to be used "all the week after", but that note does not prevent the Bishop authorizing additional matter for days not specially provided for.

2. THE SERMON

Sermon.—The rubric "Then shall follow the Sermon" does not mean that there must be a sermon at every Eucharist; it means that this is the place for *the* Sermon, and the occasion of the Sermon is fixed by Canon 45— "one Sermon every Sunday of the year."[1] Thus, no Sermon is required at the Holy-day Eucharist, nor at any other additional Eucharist. On the other hand, the Canon is not to be taken as forbidding the preaching of more than one Sermon a week. Another Canon of 1604, the 55th, orders a Bidding Prayer to be used before all Sermons, Lectures, and Homilies.

3 WARNING OF COMMUNION

Clearly the Sunday before Easter is one of the occasions when notice should be given of Communion; and when the minister gives such warning, he must read the First or Second Exhortation. It is important that one should be read at least three times a year, since three times must all

[1] The Scottish Liturgy makes this still more clear : " If there be a Sermon, it followeth here "

M

the faithful communicate ; and such occasions would naturally be the Sundays before Christmas and Whitsunday, in
addition to Palm Sunday. There is, however, no obligation
to read these Exhortations every Sunday. The same applies
to the Third Exhortation ("Dearly beloved in the Lord,")
which ought certainly to be read on occasion ; there can be
no justification for its omission on any Celebration at Easter,
while it ought to be read also at all communions on such days
as Christmas and Whitsunday. It is full of valuable teaching,
and is very beautiful, as are also the First and Second Exhortations. The First is important, since it shows clearly
that the ministry of reconciliation is offered to all and enforced
on none.

The rubrics at the beginning of the Communion Service
are also of great importance, and their neglect has led to
many evils. Without them there is nothing to prevent a
Turk or an infidel, from approaching the Table of the Lord ;
the greatest means for the reconciliation of enemies and
the promotion of fellowship is lost ; and the parish priest
loses his best chance of training the newly confirmed in the
habits of regular Communion, and (in much-frequented
churches) of knowing who his people are. He also loses
his chance of seeing that there are communicants at every
Eucharist.

But rubrics have to be revived tactfully and gradually,
and with careful explanation that the thing is done because
the Prayer Book orders it. At first the parson may find it
sufficient to ask for the names before Easter : in the villages
he will probably have to do this at first by asking verbally
those who ought to come. But in town parishes he will
generally find it better to put pencils and slips of paper on
a table at the west end of the church, and to ask the people
to write their names, and put the slips in the "Vicar's Box"
(a box with a lock, a slit in the top for letters, and a piece of
glass let into the front)—for every church will need such
a table and box. Slips may be printed in such form as
this : "I intend, God willing, to make my Communion
next Sunday at . . . o'clock. *Name* . . . *Address* . . . But
plain slips may be made (e.g. eight can be made out of

a sheet of notepaper), and people asked to write their names and addresses and to put the hour of service in the corner.

It is really essential that this be done before Easter—i.e., on Palm Sunday, the warning having been given in the appointed Exhortation, and the slips remaining on the table throughout Holy Week. In subsequent years it can be done also on the Sundays before Christmas and Whitsunday; and there is no difficulty in securing its constant observance, as time goes on—those who communicate weekly or monthly telling the priest once for all each Easter (for which purpose a sentence might be added where a printed form is used—"And on every Sunday and Holy-day (or every Sunday), or the —— Sunday in each month,") and only making a special notification in case of absence. The parish priest can teach his Confirmation candidates to do this. For them, and for others, it will be of the nature of a promise; and they will learn the forgotten duty of regular Communion and of living Christian lives as befits communicants. For the priest himself it will provide a religious chart of his parish; he will know who is dropping off, whom to warn, whom to encourage, whom specially to pray for.

He should not increase the number of Celebrations until he is assured in this way that there will be in all reasonable probability "a convenient number to communicate," "according to his discretion," "three at the least." It is dangerous to forget these rubrics; for the compilers of the Prayer Book undoubtedly wished to restore the primitive custom of frequent Communion, by destroying the practice of solitary Masses without communicants (which was indeed also condemned by the Council of Trent), and they were undoubtedly right in doing so. Frequent Communion with the proper dispositions is the secret of a holy life, and is as necessary for the laity as for the clergy. For this very reason the practice of stopping a duly announced Celebration at the last moment because there happens to be less than three communicants, is nothing less than disastrous. This is to put the letter of a rubric before the spirit of the

Gospel; and even the rubrics, taken together, seem to require such action, if it is necessary, to be taken "at least some time the day before."

4. THE COMMUNION AND THE COMMUNICANTS

Many clergy find it useful from time to time to post directions for communicants on the notice board or to print them in the parish magazine, since ignorance on the subject is exceedingly widespread; and all find something of the kind necessary in preparing Confirmation candidates. The following suggestions may be found useful for these purposes:

1. All are helped in their devotions if everything at the Communion goes smoothly, without delay or uncertainty Therefore, *as the priest makes his Communion*, the server gives the signal for communicants to approach [by ringing the bell, or opening the doors of the rood-screen, or the chancel-gate, or going to the side of the chancel, as the case may be]. At this signal those in front should approach the altar *at once* (having made "due and lowly reverence" on leaving their seats), and kneel at the rail, so as to be in readiness when the priest turns round.

2. They will be followed by those immediately behind them, who will go and kneel (or stand, in the case of older people) in the chancel ready to fill their places at the rail

3. Those behind the second party will remain in their seats until the majority of the second party have gone to the rail: they will then go up and fill their place in the chancel. Thus there will always be a railful of people, and there will always be some waiting in the chancel to take their places, so as to avoid all chance of delay. But *there will be no one standing about in the body of the church*: the alleys will be clear, and those who are waiting their turn will be kneeling quietly at prayer in their seats. Great opportunities of worship are thus saved, and much worry avoided.

4. The communicant waiting in the chancel will go and kneel in the first vacant place at the rail on his side. He will kneel upright, because any bending of the head or body

adds to the labour and difficulty of the minister more than perhaps would be imagined.

5. When the priest approaches, the communicant will hold out his hands as high as convenient, i e. about the level of his chest, the palms being open and the fingers closed, the back of the right hand resting on the palm of the left, after the manner of the early Church. He thus receives the Sacrament, not in one hand nor in the fingers, but, as the rubric directs, "into their hands." He then raises it, without waiting, to his mouth. (In the Scottish rite the rubric directs the communicant to say *Amen* at the administration of each kind.)

6. When the deacon approaches with the chalice, the communicant takes it *firmly* in both hands, grasping the base with his right hand and the stem with his left. He then immediately raises it to his lips and drinks a few drops of the Sacrament of our Lord's Blood. He should not wait till the words of administration are half-through, but should take the chalice at the beginning of the words and drink at once while the words are being said; for this prevents delay, and it must be remembered that the words "Drink this," etc., are not the command to drink (which is conveyed by the opening words, "The Blood of our Lord," etc.), but are the explanation of the spirit in which we are to drink, the emphasis being "Drink this *in remembrance that* Christ died for thee" (without a comma) and not *"Drink this,* in remembrance that Christ died for thee."

7. The communicant remains kneeling while the brother on his left is receiving the chalice, so as to avoid disturbing him. When that is over, he rises and goes quietly to his seat, without making any further reverence.

8. As he has spent in earnest preparation the time before his turn arrived, so, after he has come back to his seat, he will devote the remaining moments to thanksgiving. And it is well, if he is able, to remain some minutes in church after the service is over, devoting himself to thanksgiving, meditation, and resolutions for the future.

THE ALCUIN CLUB

Founded with the object of promoting the study of the History and
use of the Book of Common Prayer.

Committee

ATHELSTAN RILEY, Esq., Sr., M.A., *Chairman.*

E. G. CUTHBERT F. ATCHLEY,
Esq., L.R.C.P., M.R.C.S.

W. J. BIRKBECK, Esq., M.A.,
F.S.A.

Rev. Prebendary F. E. BRIGHTMAN,
M.A.

Rev. A. L. COATES, M.A.

Rev. PERCY DEARMER, D.D.

F. C. EELES, Esq., F.R.Hist.S.,
F.S.A.Scot.

Rev. W. HOWARD FRERE, D.D.

W. H. ST. JOHN HOPE, Esq., M.A.

HAROLD C. KING, Esq., M.A.

Rev. T. A. LACEY, M.A.

Rev. J. N. NEWLAND-SMITH, M.A.

Rev. CHR. WORDSWORTH, M.A.

Hon. Secretary and Treasurer

REV. PERCY DEARMER, D.D., 102 Adelaide Road, London, N.W.

Clerk to the Committee

MISS WARD, 102 Adelaide Road, London, N.W.

Bankers

THE LONDON AND PROVINCIAL BANK, 55 England's Lane, London, N.W.

Hon. Auditors

Messrs. MCAULIFFE, DAVIS and HOPE.

THE ALCUIN CLUB

THE ALCUIN CLUB has been formed to encourage and assist in the practical study of ceremonial, and the arrangement of Churches, their furniture and ornaments, in accordance with the rubrics of the Book of Common Prayer, strict obedience to which is the guiding principle of the work of the Club

The Club consists of Members and Associates, who must be in communion with the Church of England

The Subscription for Members is 20s per annum, entitling them to all publications *gratis*, and for Associates 2s 6d per annum, entitling them to such of the Tracts *gratis*, and such reductions on other publications as the Committee may determine

Applications for election should be sent to the Honorary Secretary, or one of the Committee

The Annual Report and List of Members will be sent to any one on application to the Honorary Secretary

RULES

1 The object of THE ALCUIN CLUB shall be the promotion of the study of the history and use of the Book of Common Prayer

2 The Work of the Club shall be the publication of Tracts dealing with the Object of the Club, and such other works as may seem desirable, with reproductions of miniatures from MSS, and photographs of Church Furniture, Ornaments and Vestments

3 The Club shall consist of Members and Associates, to be elected by the Committee, all Members and Associates to be in communion with the Church of England

4. The subscription for Members shall be 20s per annum, entitling them to all publications *gratis*, and for Associates 2s 6d per annum, entitling them to such of the Tracts *gratis*, and such reductions on other publications as the Committee may determine There shall be no Entrance Fee nor Composition for Subscriptions

5 The affairs of the Club shall be managed by a Chairman and a Committee of not more than twenty Members or Associates, to be elected by Members of the Club, and subject as to one-fifth, to retirement by rotation annually

6 A General Meeting of the Club shall be held every year on May 19th (the anniversary of the death of Alcuin), for the purpose of receiving a Report from the Committee, electing Committee-men, and transacting the general business of the Club

7 A General Meeting of the Club may be called at any time by the Chairman or five Members of the Committee

8 The Chairman, Treasurer and Secretary shall be elected by the Committee from among their number

9 No alteration shall be made in the rules of the Club except at a General Meeting of the Members, seven days' notice of the proposed change having been sent beforehand to all Members of the Club

. Persons wishing to join the Club are requested to communicate with the Hon Secretary, 102 Adelaide Road, London, N W, who will send full information

PUBLICATIONS

COLLECTIONS

I   **English Altars.** A large folio volume with 14 pp of Collotypes Explanatory Notes by W H St John Hope, Esq , M A
[Out of print.]

Price £1 10s   Issued to Members for 1897-8

II   **Exposition de la Messe.** A large folio volume containing a Treatise on the Mass from a French version of the Legenda Aurea of Jacobus de Voragine, now in the Fitzwilliam Museum at Cambridge, and 22 plates from Illustrations in this MS   Together with four Tracts from "The Lay Folks' Mass Book," "Merita Missæ," etc. Edited by Rev WALTER HOWARD FRERE, D D

Price £1 10s.   Issued to Members for 1898-9

III and IV   **Pontifical Services,** vols. 1 and 11   Two large folio volumes containing Descriptive Notes and a Liturgical Introduction by Rev WALTER HOWARD FRERE, D D , and 20 plates of 62 Illustrations from Miniatures of the XVth and XVIth centuries

Price £1 10s each   Issued to Members for 1899-1900 and Dec. 31, 1900.

V   **Dat Boexken vander Missen.** (The Booklet of the Mass) By GHERIT VANDER GOUDE, 1507   34 woodcuts illustrating the Celebration of the Holy Communion, described, and the explanatory text of the Flemish original translated, with illustrative excerpts from contemporary missals and tracts, by the Rev PERCY DEARMER, D D

Price £1 1s   Issued to Members for 1900-1 and Associates for 1898-1901

VI   **The Edwardian Inventories for Bedfordshire.** Edited by F C EELES, F S A Scot , from transcripts by the Rev J E BROWN, B A

Price 5s   Issued to Members for 1900-1

VII   **The Edwardian Inventories for Huntingdonshire.** Edited by Mrs S C LOMAS, editor of "State Papers Charles I Addenda," etc , from transcripts by T. CRAIB

Price 10s   Issued to Members for 1900-1

VIII   **Pontifical Services,** vol 111   Descriptive notes and 143 Illustrations from woodcuts in pontificals of the XVIth century Edited by F. C EELES, F R Hist.S , F S A Scot.

Price £1 1s   Issued to Members for 1902.

IX   **The Edwardian Inventories for Buckinghamshire.** Edited by F C EELES, F R Hist S , F S A Scot , from transcripts by the Rev J. E BROWN, B A.

Price £1 1s   Issued to Members for 1903.

FORTHCOMING PUBLICATIONS

Further Collections will be selected from the following .—

The following Tracts are also proposed —

REDUCED PRICES FOR MEMBERS

₊ Members and Associates may obtain copies of the Collections
and Tracts at a reduced price *through the Hon Secretary.* The price of
the first ten Collections is now reduced to one third.

REDUCED PRICES OF COLLECTIONS

II, III, IV	-	-	-	-	-	£0	10	0	each
V, VIII, IX, X	-	-	-	-		0	7	0	,,
VII	-	-	-	-	-	0	3	4	,,
XII, XVII	-	-	-	-		0	12	10	,,
VI	-	-	-	-	-	0	1	8	,,
XVIII	-	-	-	-		0	4	6	,,
XIII	-	-	-	-	-	2	4	0	,,
XIV, XV, XVI, the set of three			-			3	0	0	

REDUCED PRICES OF TRACTS

					s	*d*
Ornaments of the Rubric	-	-	-		3	6
Consolidation	-	-	-	-	0	8
A First English Ordo	-	-	-	-	1	10
Ditto (in boards)	-	-	-	-	0	9
The People's Prayers	-	-	-	-	1	0
Ditto (in paper covers)	-	-	-	-	0	5
The Sign of the Cross	-	-	-	-	1	0
The "Interpretations" of the Elizabethan Bishops	-	-	-	-	1	0

LANTERN SLIDES

Slides may be hired from the Hon Sec, 102 Adelaide Road, N W,
at a charge of 3s. each set, with 1s. for insurance and postage. The
subjects are —

1 The Ornaments Rubric (For Notes, F C Eeles, *The Ornaments Rubric* 1d)
2 The Ornaments of the Ministers (For Notes, Percy Dearmer, *The Ornaments of the Ministers* 1s 6d)
3 The Chancel and the Holy Table (For Notes, Harold C King, *The Chancel and Altar* 1s 6d)
4 Illustrations of the Liturgy (For Notes, Alcuin Club Collection, XIX)

Publishers Messrs. A R Mowbray & Co Ltd
28 Margaret Street, London, W, and 9 High Street, Oxford

493008

Printed by A. R. Mowbray & Co Ltd.
London and Oxford

Milton Keynes UK
Ingram Content Group UK Ltd.
UKHW022229310823
427872UK00005B/75